PEMDAS

Parentheses first, then **Exponents**, then **Multiplication** and **Division** (left to right), and lastly **Addition** and **Subtraction** (left to right).

Median and Mode

The median is the **value that falls in the middle of the set**.

The mode is the **value that appears most often**.

Counting the Possibilities

If there are **m ways** one event can happen and **n ways** a second event can happen, then there are **$m \times n$ ways** for the 2 events to happen.

ESSENTIAL FORMULAS

Average Rate Formula

Average A per B $= \dfrac{\text{Total } A}{\text{Total } B}$

Average Speed $= \dfrac{\text{Total distance}}{\text{Total time}}$

Percent Formula

Part = Percent × Whole

Average Formula

Average $= \dfrac{\text{Sum of the terms}}{\text{Number of terms}}$

Probability Formula

Probability $= \dfrac{\text{Favorable Outcomes}}{\text{Total Possible Outcomes}}$

Multiplying and Dividing Powers

To multiply powers with the same base, **add the exponents and keep the same base**.

To divide powers with the same base, **subtract the exponents and keep the same base**.

Raising Powers to Powers

To raise a power to a power, **multiply the exponents**.

Negative Exponent and Rational Exponent

$x^{-n} = \dfrac{1}{x^n}$ $x^{\frac{1}{n}} = \sqrt[n]{x}$

Direct and Inverse Variation

In direct variation, $y = kx$, where k is a nonzero constant.
In inverse variation, $xy = k$, where k is a constant.

Domain and Range of a Function

The domain of a function is the set of values for which the function is defined.

Determining Absolute Value

The absolute value of a number is the distance of the number from zero on the number line.

Multiplying Binomials—FOIL

To multiply binomials, use **FOIL**. First multiply the **F**irst terms. Next the **O**uter terms. Then the **I**nner terms. And finally the **L**ast terms. Then add and combine like terms.

Factoring the Difference of Squares

$a^2 - b^2 = (a - b)(a + b)$

Factoring the Square of a Binomial

$a^2 + 2ab + b^2 = (a + b)^2$ $a^2 - 2ab + b^2 = (a - b)^2$

Quadratic Equation

$ax^2 + bx + c = 0$

Finding the Distance Between Two Points

$d = \sqrt{(x_1 - x_2)^2 + (y_1 - y_2)^2}$

Solving an Inequality

When you **multiply or divide both sides by a negative number**, you must **reverse the sign**.

Using Two Points to Find the Slope

Slope $= \dfrac{\text{Change in } y}{\text{Change in } x} = \dfrac{\text{Rise}}{\text{Run}}$

Using an Equation to Find the Slope (slope-intercept)

$y = mx + b$

Finding the Midpoint

If the endpoints are (x_1, y_1) and (x_2, y_2), the midpoint is:

$\left(\dfrac{(x_1 + x_2)}{2}, \dfrac{(y_1 + y_2)}{2} \right)$

Intersecting Lines

When two lines intersect, **adjacent angles are supplementary and vertical angles are equal**.

Kaplan's 5-step Method for Quantitative Comparisons

Step 1. Compare piece by piece.
Step 2. Make one column look like the other.
Step 3. Do the same thing to both columns.
Step 4. Pick numbers.
Step 5. Redraw the diagram.

GEOMETRY

Interior and Exterior Angles of a Triangle

The 3 angles of any triangle **add up to 180 degrees**.
The 3 exterior angles of a triangle add up to **360 degrees**.

Area of a Triangle

Area of Triangle $= \frac{1}{2}$(base)(height)

Pythagorean Theorem

For all right triangles: $(\text{leg}_1)^2 + (\text{leg}_2)^2 = (\text{hypotenuse})^2$

Special Right Triangles

The 3-4-5 Triangle
The 30-60-90 Triangle
The 5-12-13 Triangle
The 45-45-90 Triangle

Area of a Rectangle

Area of Rectangle = length × width

Area of a Parallelogram

Area of Parallelogram = base × height

Area of a Square

Area of Square $= (\text{side})^2$

Circumference of a Circle

Circumference $= 2\pi r$

Length of an Arc

If n is the degree measure of the arc's central angle, then the formula is:

Length of an Arc $= 1(\frac{n}{360})(2\pi r)$

Area of a Circle

Area of a Circle $= \pi r^2$

Area of a Sector

If n is the degree measure of the sector's central angle, then the formula is:

Area of a Sector $= 1(\frac{n}{360})(\pi r^2)$

Interior Angles of a Polygon

The sum of the measures of the interior angles of a polygon $= (n - 2) \times 180$, where n is the number of sides.

Surface Area of a Rectangular Solid

Surface Area $= 2lw + 2wh + 2lh$

Volume of a Rectangular Solid

Volume of a Rectangular Solid $= lwh$
Volume of a Cube $= \ell^3$

Volume of a Cylinder

Volume of a Cylinder $= \pi r^2 h$

KAPLAN
Test Prep and Admissions
kaptest.com

GRE Verbal Skills

4-step Method for Reading Comprehension

Step 1: Attack the first third of the question.

Step 2: Create a mental roadmap.

Step 3: Stop to sum up.

Step 4: Attack the questions.

4-step Method for Sentence Completions

Step 1: Read for clue words.

Step 2: Predict the answer.

Step 3: Select the best match.

Step 4: Read your selection in the sentence.

ANALOGY TIPS

4-step Method for Analogies

Step 1: Find a strong bridge between the stem words.

Step 2: Plug the answer choices into the bridge.

Step 3: Adjust the bridge as necessary.

Step 4: Eliminate all answer choices with weak bridges. If two choices have the same bridge, eliminate them both.

5 Classic Analogy Bridges

1. Definition
   Example: PLATITUDE : TRITE
2. Function/purpose
   Example: MONEY : VAULT
3. Lack
   Example: LUCID : OBSCURITY
4. Characteristic actions/items
   Example: PIROUETTE : DANCER
5. Degree (often to an extreme)
   Example: ATTENTIVE: RAPT

4-step Method for Antonyms

Step 1: Define the root word.

Step 2: Reverse it by thinking about the word's opposite.

Step 3: Find the choice that matches your preconceived notion of the choice.

Step 4: Eliminate any choices you can and guess among those remaining.

ESSAY-WRITING (AWA) SKILLS

WORD ROOT LIST

If you don't have much time to spend on vocabulary, word roots can get you through the most commonly tested GRE words. Here are some samples:

A, AN—not, without
• amoral, anarchy

AC, ACR—sharp, sour
• acute, acrid

AMBI, AMPHI—both
• ambiguous, amphibious

AMBL, AMBUL—walk
• amble, ambulatory

AUD—hear
• audio

BENE, BEN—good
• benefactor, benign

BIO—life
• biology

CARN—flesh
• carnage

CEDE, CESS—yield, go
• cessation, secede

CO, COM, CON—with, together
• cogent, compliant, consensus

CURR, CURS—run
• current, precursor

DE—down, out, apart
• debilitate, deride

DEMO, DEM—people
• democrat, demagogue

DUC, DUCT—lead
• induce, conduct

EGO—self
• egoist

EN, EM—in, into
• enter, embroil

EU—well, good
• euphemism

FAL, FALS—deceive
• infallible, false

FORE—before
• forecast

FRAG, FRAC—break
• fragment, fracture

GRAPH, GRAM—writing
• biography, grammar

GRAT—pleasing
• gratitude

HELIO, HELI—sun
• heliocentric, perihelion

HOL—whole
• holocaust

INTRA, INTR—within
• intravenous, intrinsic

JECT, JET—throw
• trajectory, jettison

JUD—judge
• judicious

LAT—side
• lateral

LING, LANG—tongue
• lingo, language

MACRO—great
• macrocosm

MAL—bad
• maladroit

MEM, MIN—remember
• memento, reminisce

MIT, MISS—send
• transmit, missive

NAU, NAV—ship, sailor
• nautical, circumnavigate

NEO—new
• neoclassical

OB—against
• obsequious

OMNI—all
• omnipotent

PAC—peace
• pacifist

PHON—sound
• phonograph

POT—drink
• potable

QUAD, QUAR, QUAT—four
• quadrant, quarantine, quaternary

QUIE—quiet
• acquiesce

RETRO—backward
• retrospective

RID, RIS—laugh
• ridiculous, derision

SED, SID—sit
• sedentary, residence

SEN—old
• senior

SYN, SYM—together
• synthesis, symbiosis

TACIT, TIC—silent
• tacit, reticent

TERM—end
• terminal

TORT—twist
• distort

TOX—poison
• toxic

UNI, UN—one
• unify, unanimous

URB—city
• urban

VAC—empty
• evacuate

VOLV, VOLUT—turn, roll
• revolve, convoluted

VOR—eat
• voracious

For an Issue Essay:

1. Take the issue apart.
• Determine the conclusion and the (offered or implied) counterconclusion.
• Consider the circumstances under which the conclusion would be true/untrue.
2. Select the points you will make.
• Decide whether to agree or disagree, naming two to four reasons.
3. Organize.
• In paragraph 1, restate the issue, agree/disagree, and state two to four reasons.
• In the next two to four paragraphs, elaborate, using evidence, testimony, and anecdotes.
• In the second-to-last paragraph, present and refute an alternative argument.
• In the last paragraph, summarize your points.
4. Type your essay.
5. Proofread.

For an Argument Essay:

1. Take the argument apart.
• Determine the conclusion, evidence, and assumptions.
• Consider the circumstances under which the assumptions are valid/invalid.
• Consider what would strengthen/weaken the argument.
2. Select the points you will make.
• Decide which weaknesses/strengths of the argument are critical, and for which of those you can marshal evidence.
3. Organize.
• In paragraph 1, demonstrate that you understand the argument, list weaknesses, and describe what could strengthen the argument.
• In paragraph 2, detail assumptions on which the argument hinges, describe what would be required to validate the assumptions, and list gaps between existing evidence and what's necessary.

• In paragraph 3, discuss poorly defined terms and their effect on the argument.
• In the last paragraph, discuss what could strengthen the argument and summarize your points.
4. Type your essay.
5. Proofread.

5 Tips for Writing a Great AWA Essay

1. Use transitional phrases.
2. Try not to misspell words.
3. Vary the structure of your sentences.
4. Vary word choice.
5. When critiquing an argument: analyze the strength of the evidence presented, point out unwarranted assumptions, and present neglected alternatives. When constructing your own argument: make your points of evidence specific and defensible, avoid unwarranted assumptions, and anticipate your opposition by providing a refutation of the strongest point against your own argument.

BORDERS.

Kaplan Publishing
Published by SIMON & SCHUSTER
Rockefeller Center
1230 Avenue of the Americas
New York, NY 10020

Executive Editor: Jennifer Farthing
Project Editor: Megan Gilbert
Production Manager: Michael Shevlin
Interior Page Design and Production: Dave Chipps
Cover Design: Cheung Tai

Manufactured in the United States of America.
Published simultaneously in Canada.

10 9 8 7 6 5 4 3 2 1

September 2005

ISBN-13: 978-0-7432-8754-8
ISBN-10:   0-7432-8754-1

For bulk sales contact your local Borders store and ask to speak to the Corporate Sales Representative.

Test Prep and Admissions

GRE®

Diagnostic Test and Practice Questions

A BORDERS EXCLUSIVE

By the Staff of Kaplan Test Prep and Admissions

Simon & Schuster

NEW YORK · LONDON · SYDNEY · TORONTO

TABLE OF CONTENTS

You are planning to take the GRE and you don't have much time. Where to begin? The first step is to assess your strengths and weaknesses, so you can focus your study time. This book helps you do just that.

Here's how to use the *GRE Diagnostic:*

Step One: Take the GRE Diagnostic Test

Take the full-length practice test—timed—as a test run for the real thing. The explanations for every question are included at the end so you can understand your mistakes.

Step Two: Identify Your Strengths and Weaknesses

Check your answers to the diagnostic, and note how many you got right and how many you got wrong. Look for patterns. Did sentence-correction questions trip you up? Did you ace the problem solving questions? Try not to limit your review only to the questions you got wrong. Instead, read all the explanations to reinforce key concepts and sharpen your skills. If necessary, go back to the questions to better understand the material and concepts on which you will be tested.

Step Three: Create a Customized Study Plan

Based on your performance on the diagnostic test and the amount of time you have available to study before the GRE, you can use the content in Section Two to create a customized study plan. Think about what you learned in Step Two about the material you need to focus your study time on. Then, realistically determine how much time you have to devote to GRE study. Use the information and tools in this section to build your plan. Then stick to it—your study plan only works for you if you follow it!

Step Four: Review to Reinforce and Build Skills

Section Three provides you with targeted quizzes to help you conquer the content you need to know to score high on the GRE. Based on your study plan, take the quizzes here to help prepare you for Test Day.

About the GRE

The GRE is a standardized test that helps graduate schools assess the qualifications of students entering into their programs. Though many factors play a role in admissions decisions, the GRE score is usually an important one. And, generally speaking, being average just won't cut it. While the median GRE score is somewhere around 500, you need a score of at least 600 to be considered competitive by the top graduate programs.

The first thing to know about the GRE is that it is a computer-adaptive test; that is, a test taken on computer at a private workstation, scheduled at your convenience at a test-center near you. In a computer-adaptive test, you see only one question at a time. And instead of having a predetermined mixture of basic, medium, and hard questions, the computer selects questions for you based on how well you are doing.

The GRE measures basic verbal, mathematical, and analytical writing skills, and contains three sections: Analytical Writing Assessment (AWA), Verbal, and Quantitative (Math). First, you'll begin with the two AWA sections—75 minutes to type two essays. Then come two multiple-choice sections: Verbal and Quantitative (Math). The Verbal section includes 30 questions in four types: Sentence Completion, Analogies, Antonyms, and Reading Comprehension. The Quantitative section contains 28 math questions in two formats: Problem Solving and Quantitative Comparison.

Overall scaled scores range between 200 and 800. Because the test is graded on a preset curve, the scaled score will correspond to a certain percentile. So an overall score of 590, let's say, corresponds to the 80th percentile, meaning that 80 percent of test takers scored at or below that same level. The percentile helps graduate school admissions officers to see where you fall in a large pool of applicants.

For complete registration information about the GRE, download the GRE Registration Bulletin from **www.gre.org**.

Section One

GRE DIAGNOSTIC TEST

CHAPTER ONE

Diagnostic Test

HOW TO TAKE THE DIAGNOSTIC TEST

Before taking the Diagnostic Test, find a quiet place where you can work uninterrupted for approximately 3 hours. Make sure you have a comfortable desk, several pencils, and some scratch paper. Time yourself according to the time limits shown at the beginning of each section. It's okay to take a short break between sections, but for the most accurate results, you should go through all three sections in one sitting.

Use the answer sheet on the following page to record your answers to the multiple-choice sections. Do not skip a question; in the actual test-taking environment you won't be able to skip from question to question. If you're having trouble figuring out the best answer, take your best guess and move on. Remember, you won't be able to go back and check your work, so choose your answers wisely. Use the lined sheets provided to write your essays, or type them into a computer.

You'll find the answer key and scoring information in chapter 2. Good luck!

GRE Diagnostic Test
Answer Sheet

Remove (or photocopy) the answer sheet and use it to complete the practice test.
See the answer key in chapter 2 when finished.

SECTION

1

Section One is the Analytical Writing Assessment.
Lined pages on which to write your essay can be found in that section.

SECTION

2

1. Ⓐ Ⓑ Ⓒ Ⓓ Ⓔ   11. Ⓐ Ⓑ Ⓒ Ⓓ Ⓔ   21. Ⓐ Ⓑ Ⓒ Ⓓ Ⓔ   31. Ⓐ Ⓑ Ⓒ Ⓓ Ⓔ
2. Ⓐ Ⓑ Ⓒ Ⓓ Ⓔ   12. Ⓐ Ⓑ Ⓒ Ⓓ Ⓔ   22. Ⓐ Ⓑ Ⓒ Ⓓ Ⓔ   32. Ⓐ Ⓑ Ⓒ Ⓓ Ⓔ
3. Ⓐ Ⓑ Ⓒ Ⓓ Ⓔ   13. Ⓐ Ⓑ Ⓒ Ⓓ Ⓔ   23. Ⓐ Ⓑ Ⓒ Ⓓ Ⓔ   33. Ⓐ Ⓑ Ⓒ Ⓓ Ⓔ
4. Ⓐ Ⓑ Ⓒ Ⓓ Ⓔ   14. Ⓐ Ⓑ Ⓒ Ⓓ Ⓔ   24. Ⓐ Ⓑ Ⓒ Ⓓ Ⓔ   34. Ⓐ Ⓑ Ⓒ Ⓓ Ⓔ
5. Ⓐ Ⓑ Ⓒ Ⓓ Ⓔ   15. Ⓐ Ⓑ Ⓒ Ⓓ Ⓔ   25. Ⓐ Ⓑ Ⓒ Ⓓ Ⓔ   35. Ⓐ Ⓑ Ⓒ Ⓓ Ⓔ
6. Ⓐ Ⓑ Ⓒ Ⓓ Ⓔ   16. Ⓐ Ⓑ Ⓒ Ⓓ Ⓔ   26. Ⓐ Ⓑ Ⓒ Ⓓ Ⓔ   36. Ⓐ Ⓑ Ⓒ Ⓓ Ⓔ
7. Ⓐ Ⓑ Ⓒ Ⓓ Ⓔ   17. Ⓐ Ⓑ Ⓒ Ⓓ Ⓔ   27. Ⓐ Ⓑ Ⓒ Ⓓ Ⓔ   37. Ⓐ Ⓑ Ⓒ Ⓓ Ⓔ
8. Ⓐ Ⓑ Ⓒ Ⓓ Ⓔ   18. Ⓐ Ⓑ Ⓒ Ⓓ Ⓔ   28. Ⓐ Ⓑ Ⓒ Ⓓ Ⓔ   38. Ⓐ Ⓑ Ⓒ Ⓓ Ⓔ
9. Ⓐ Ⓑ Ⓒ Ⓓ Ⓔ   19. Ⓐ Ⓑ Ⓒ Ⓓ Ⓔ   29. Ⓐ Ⓑ Ⓒ Ⓓ Ⓔ
10. Ⓐ Ⓑ Ⓒ Ⓓ Ⓔ   20. Ⓐ Ⓑ Ⓒ Ⓓ Ⓔ   30. Ⓐ Ⓑ Ⓒ Ⓓ Ⓔ

right in
Section 2

wrong in
Section 2

SECTION

3

39. Ⓐ Ⓑ Ⓒ Ⓓ Ⓔ   49. Ⓐ Ⓑ Ⓒ Ⓓ Ⓔ   59. Ⓐ Ⓑ Ⓒ Ⓓ Ⓔ
40. Ⓐ Ⓑ Ⓒ Ⓓ Ⓔ   50. Ⓐ Ⓑ Ⓒ Ⓓ Ⓔ   60. Ⓐ Ⓑ Ⓒ Ⓓ Ⓔ
41. Ⓐ Ⓑ Ⓒ Ⓓ Ⓔ   51. Ⓐ Ⓑ Ⓒ Ⓓ Ⓔ   61. Ⓐ Ⓑ Ⓒ Ⓓ Ⓔ
42. Ⓐ Ⓑ Ⓒ Ⓓ Ⓔ   52. Ⓐ Ⓑ Ⓒ Ⓓ Ⓔ   62. Ⓐ Ⓑ Ⓒ Ⓓ Ⓔ
43. Ⓐ Ⓑ Ⓒ Ⓓ Ⓔ   53. Ⓐ Ⓑ Ⓒ Ⓓ Ⓔ   63. Ⓐ Ⓑ Ⓒ Ⓓ Ⓔ
44. Ⓐ Ⓑ Ⓒ Ⓓ Ⓔ   54. Ⓐ Ⓑ Ⓒ Ⓓ Ⓔ   64. Ⓐ Ⓑ Ⓒ Ⓓ Ⓔ
45. Ⓐ Ⓑ Ⓒ Ⓓ Ⓔ   55. Ⓐ Ⓑ Ⓒ Ⓓ Ⓔ   65. Ⓐ Ⓑ Ⓒ Ⓓ Ⓔ
46. Ⓐ Ⓑ Ⓒ Ⓓ Ⓔ   56. Ⓐ Ⓑ Ⓒ Ⓓ Ⓔ   66. Ⓐ Ⓑ Ⓒ Ⓓ Ⓔ
47. Ⓐ Ⓑ Ⓒ Ⓓ Ⓔ   57. Ⓐ Ⓑ Ⓒ Ⓓ Ⓔ   67. Ⓐ Ⓑ Ⓒ Ⓓ Ⓔ
48. Ⓐ Ⓑ Ⓒ Ⓓ Ⓔ   58. Ⓐ Ⓑ Ⓒ Ⓓ Ⓔ   68. Ⓐ Ⓑ Ⓒ Ⓓ Ⓔ

right in
Section 3

wrong in
Section 3

SECTION 1: ANALYTICAL WRITING

Total Questions: 2

Time: 75 Minutes

Present Your Perspective on an Issue:

Time: 45 Minutes

Present your perspective on the issue below, using relevant reasons and/or examples to support your views.

> "Every e-mail originating from an unknown user may contain a virus. Companies should maintain active vigilance to prevent employees from opening e-mails that are from unknown users."

_____

_____

_____

_____

_____

_____

_____

_____

_____

_____

_____

_____

_____

_____

_____

_____

_____

_____

_____

_____

_____

_____

_____

_____

_____

_____

_____

_____

_____

Analysis of an Argument:

Time: 30 Minutes

Discuss how well reasoned you find this argument.

The following appeared in a letter to the editor of a local newspaper:

"Television cartoons portray an unrealistic image of violence. All too often, one cartoon character uses dangerous implements to inflict bodily harm on another, and the effects of this violence upon the other character are completely negligible. If our children were to imitate this behavior, it would be catastrophic. Therefore, all cartoons should revolve around non-violent conflicts, and all violent children's programming should be banned from the networks."

_____

_____

_____

_____

_____

_____

_____

_____

_____

_____

SECTION 2: VERBAL

Total Questions: 38

Time: 30 Minutes

Directions: Each of the following questions begins with a sentence that has either one or two blanks. The blanks indicate that a piece of the sentence is missing. Each sentence is followed by five answer choices that consist of words or phrases. Select the answer choice that best completes the sentence.

1. The ecological balance of the park's natural hot springs has become increasingly _____, most frequently because of human disruption.

    (A) understood

    (B) unstable

    (C) observed

    (D) contaminated

    (E) accelerated

2. It is _____ that the novelist wrote so eloquently about life on the Lower East Side of Manhattan in the early twentieth century since he was born in 1946 and raised in a Midwestern suburb until the age of 24.

    (A) doubtful

    (B) natural

    (C) surprising

    (D) worrying

    (E) laughable

3. Physics, like economics, concerns itself with the maintenance of _____ through complex balances of actions and reactions.

    (A) equilibrium

    (B) goods

    (C) inertia

    (D) benefits

    (E) value

4. As a culture we have become increasingly _____ the _____ effect of corporal punishment; we no longer feel that it dissuades potential criminals from breaking the law.

    (A) convinced of..economic

    (B) embroiled in..dehumanizing

    (C) skeptical of..deterrent

    (D) reliant upon..political

    (E) empowered by..strengthening

5. Disagreement over the appropriate use of force has been one of the consistent issues in international relations over time; therefore, it may be presumptuous to suggest that current international disagreements over the use of force are _____.

    (A) spurious

    (B) unique

    (C) relevant

    (D) perennial

    (E) irresolvable

6. Emotion often seems to _____ logic in heated arguments, with both parties _____ feelings rather than facts.

   (A) destroy..ignoring

   (B) trump..appealing to

   (C) empower..submitting to

   (D) display..referring to

   (E) equal..confusing

7. Greek tragedies, which presented horrific crimes perpetrated by humans against one another and punishments for those crimes meted out by divine forces, were popular precisely because they offered audiences opportunities to consider their _____ to their _____.

   (A) obeisance..gods

   (B) duties..compatriots

   (C) allegiance..communities

   (D) responsibilities..ancestors

   (E) opposition..governments

Directions: Select the pair of words that expresses a relationship most similar to a relationship expressed in the original pair of words.

8. ASCETIC : AUSTERE ::

   (A) adolescent : mature

   (B) rustic : spartan

   (C) disciple : reverent

   (D) warrior : martial

   (E) zealot : fervent

9. SCALPEL : SURGEON ::

   (A) soldier : bayonet

   (B) anvil : blacksmith

   (C) shears : gardener

   (D) wrench : mechanic

   (E) camera : photographer

10. PROLOGUE : NOVEL ::

    (A) slogan : billboard

    (B) name : dogtag

    (C) scene : play

    (D) seal : wax

    (E) overture : opera

KAPLAN

11. AMBLE : WALK ::

   (A) look : stare

   (B) frown : scowl

   (C) tack : sail

   (D) wander : travel

   (E) speak : yell

12. ACORN : OAK ::

   (A) pine : needle

   (B) ivy : wall

   (C) moss : tree

   (D) almond : nut

   (E) grape : vine

13. PLEASE : ENRAPTURE ::

   (A) describe : ensure

   (B) ebb : wane

   (C) charm : beguile

   (D) appear : resolve

   (E) bemoan : regret

14. COUNTERMAND : ORDER ::

   (A) delay : conference

   (B) revoke : permission

   (C) deviate : course

   (D) retire : debt

   (E) elevate : position

15. MASTICATE : TEETH ::

   (A) leap : feet

   (B) metabolize : digestion

   (C) file : nails

   (D) grind : millstone

   (E) crack : chestnut

16. LIMERICK : POETRY ::

   (A) radio : television

   (B) conspiracy : ruse

   (C) farce : satire

   (D) midway : fair

   (E) caricature : portraiture

Directions: Answer each question based on what is stated or implied in the passage preceding the question.

Controversy has surrounded the utility and efficacy of intelligence tests since their very inception. Intelligence tests produce a
Line quantitative score known as the intelligence
5 quotient (IQ). IQ scores primarily serve as an evaluation of an individual's cognitive ability and potential. Opponents of testing argue that the intelligence quotient may not provide an accurate picture of an individual's skills. Test
10 questions do not measure social abilities, but assess only minimally the types of thought and behavior required for real life situations. Because the scoring guides are standardized, extremely imaginative or original answers may
15 fail to accrue deserved points. Although scores can serve as valuable indices of potential and ability, they may also reflect personal attitudes and test-taking sophistication. Lastly, because of the value placed on IQ scores, intelligence tests
20 administered by unqualified or disinterested individuals have the potential to damage or grossly alter a client's life. For example, testers who fail to consider such factors as an individual's socioeconomic status, ethnicity,
25 current health, and family circumstances may not understand the motivations behind certain responses. In the worst case scenario, poor test administrators may mistake a hearing, speech, or vision impediment for signs of retardation
30 or low IQ.

Nonetheless, if intelligence tests are administered and interpreted correctly, they are invaluable sources of information about an individual. They provide objective, quantitative
35 scores that allow us to compare individuals in equivalent ways. In addition, they generate a measure of individual ability that remains constant over time. Furthermore, intelligence scores may reveal hidden strengths or
40 weaknesses in individuals. This, in turn, allows us to understand and provide better treatment options, educational opportunities, and special programs for individuals. IQ scores also may be used to track the effectiveness of such programs
45 longitudinally. The merits of the Head Start program, for example, were first realized by examining the increase in IQ scores of participants. However, perhaps the most salient argument for intelligence tests is that they
50 eliminate subjective criteria and potential biases from an evaluation process. It is only through intelligence tests that psychologists and educators are able to gain essential information about a person's current cognitive functioning.

17. Which of the following best describes the organization of the passage?

(A) A scientific hypothesis is presented and dismissed as inadequate.

(B) Two competing schools of thought are discussed, then unified through theoretical analysis.

(C) A cognitively-based phenomenon is described through systematic observation.

(D) The merits of an argument are considered, then rejected in favor of the opposing position.

(E) A paradox is presented and resolved through scientific evidence.

18. Why does the author refer to individual factors in lines 22–25?

    I. To emphasize the breadth of domains affecting IQ scores.

    II. To illustrate conceivable pitfalls of poor test interpretation.

    III. To explicate the potential psychological damage of labeling children based on IQ scores.

    (A) I only

    (B) II only

    (C) III only

    (D) I and II

    (E) II and III

19. Opponents of intelligence testing would most likely agree with which of the following statements:

    (A) Intelligence tests should incorporate some assessment of social skills and pragmatic thought.

    (B) Test scores should never be used in evaluating individuals.

    (C) Creative answers are superior to those in the scoring guide.

    (D) Intelligence scores may reflect a wide variety of genetic and environmental effects.

    (E) Most administrators of IQ tests are not qualified to interpret the results.

20. What is the purpose of this passage?

    (A) To describe the damage done by poor test administrators.

    (B) To argue for the efficacy of IQ testing despite potential sources of inaccuracy.

    (C) To explain the administration of IQ tests and point out the flaws in the system.

    (D) To attack the current standard criteria for the interpretation of IQ tests.

    (E) To contradict the groundless assertions of the opponents of IQ testing.

21. Which of the following does the author NOT mention as a benefit of IQ testing?

    (A) Objective, quantitative scores that allow the comparison of individuals in equivalent ways.

    (B) The elimination of subjective criteria and potential biases from evaluation processes.

    (C) Immediate recognition of hearing, speech, or vision impediments to testing.

    (D) The revelation of an individual's hidden strengths and weaknesses.

    (E) The generation of a measure of individual ability that remains constant over time.

22. The mention of "poor test administrators" as an argument against IQ testing makes the assumption that:

    (A) Many test administrators are disinterested and attempt to sabotage results.

    (B) IQ tests are nearly impossible to administer correctly.

    (C) Test takers should never trust a test administrator.

    (D) The test administrator as well as the test taker can have a significant effect on the outcome of an IQ test.

    (E) The inherent biases of all IQ tests can always be countered by qualified test administrators.

23. Based on the passage, "test-taking sophistication"(line 18) must mean:

    (A) A person's familiarity with the procedures of standardized testing independent of the specific content of the test.

    (B) A person's high level of intelligence that makes any type of testing situation agreeable.

    (C) A person's ability to perform well under the pressure of standardized testing.

    (D) A person's acquired knowledge of art and literature available only to the very wealthy.

    (E) A person's accumulated life experience pertaining to the specific type of questions appearing in standardized tests.

The works of the major Latin and Greek writers, once central to a basic education, are now seldom read, even in translation. Many *Line* argue that this change is for the better, because 5 the ancient authors lack currency and writers who reflect today's reality are more deserving of our attention. This argument, ultimately, is shortsighted.

Those academics and scholars who 10 support the decentralization of classical texts seldom argue that the texts are completely irrelevant or otherwise lack value; they simply believe that more recent texts are more important and engaging. They argue that every 15 student should read works of this century, works by women, and works by writers from a variety of ethnic, religious, and cultural backgrounds. Their argument is convincing.

However, advocates of this position fail to 20 see that knowledge of the classics remains essential for an informed reading of even the most contemporary authors, as all western literature takes the form of permutations on a few general themes that were first – and perhaps 25 best – explicated by Latin and Greek writers. What's needed is a balance. Students should be encouraged to supplement their reading of recent authors with an in-depth study of the ancients. The one activity should reinforce, aid, 30 and inform the other. In fact, I believe that as readers (no matter what their background, race, or gender) become more familiar with the ancients, they are certain to be surprised at how relevant the ancient Latin and Greek writers are 35 today.

24. The author is primarily concerned with

(A) defending a commonly-held position

(B) challenging a school of literary criticism that emphasizes the importance of Latin and Greek authors

(C) advocating a change in the curriculum of a field of study

(D) explaining why certain authors are read more than other authors

(E) arguing that students of literature need to study Latin and Greek authors above all others

25. The passage suggests that the author would be most likely to agree with which of the following statements?

(A) The study of literature requires an extensive knowledge of only ancient authors.

(B) Reading ancient authors, while important, does not help a student understand contemporary literature.

(C) Students should always study both Latin and Greek.

(D) Studying Latin is probably less important than studying a contemporary language like French or Spanish.

(E) A complete understanding of literature is aided by knowledge of writers from the distant past.

26. The primary purpose of the second paragraph is to

   (A) explain why many thinkers are in favor of ancient authors having a relatively minor presence in the academic world

   (B) prove that ancient authors are still important, even though they aren't read as often as they once were

   (C) state the author's main idea and then defend it against critics

   (D) identify a flaw in the position that the author is arguing against

   (E) argue that contemporary authors are impossible to understand without a solid background in the classics

27. It can be inferred from the passage that Latin and Greek authors

   (A) explored many of the same themes as contemporary writers

   (B) were not widely read until the last one hundred years

   (C) are important only to those who want to understand how literature changes over time

   (D) are always superior to writers who are living today

   (E) can never appeal to all backgrounds, races, or both genders

Directions: Each of the following questions begins with a single word in capital letters. Five answer choices follow. Select the answer choice that has the most opposite meaning of the word in capital letters.

28. MANDATORY :

   (A) daily

   (B) optional

   (C) nugatory

   (D) boring

   (E) calm

29. LAMBASTE :

   (A) enervate

   (B) cook

   (C) censure

   (D) praise

   (E) discuss

30. OSCILLATE :

   (A) remain constant

   (B) move quickly

   (C) turn slowly

   (D) look around

   (E) speak quietly

31. RANCOR :

    (A) neutrality

    (B) bellicosity

    (C) peacefulness

    (D) trepidation

    (E) friendship

32. SUPPLIANT :

    (A) forgiving

    (B) inappropriate

    (C) starving

    (D) self-sufficient

    (E) inflexible

33. DEBASE :

    (A) alleviate

    (B) embark

    (C) evaluate

    (D) honor

    (E) cheapen

34. PENURY :

    (A) righteousness

    (B) fastidiousness

    (C) affluence

    (D) charm

    (E) boldness

35. ABROGATE :

    (A) ratify

    (B) espouse

    (C) compromise

    (D) annul

    (E) question

36. BECOMING :

    (A) vainglorious

    (B) unseemly

    (C) decorous

    (D) carefully composed

    (E) readily available

37. CODA :

    (A) footnote

    (B) epilogue

    (C) apostrophe

    (D) refrain

    (E) preamble

38. SMARMY :

    (A) lascivious

    (B) earnest

    (C) clean-shaven

    (D) erudite

    (E) smug

SECTION 3: QUANTITATIVE

Total Questions: 30

Time: 30 Minutes

Directions for Questions 39-53: Compare the quantities in Column A and Column B, and choose

(A) if the quantity in Column A is greater than the quantity in Column B

(B) if the quantity in Column B is greater than the quantity in Column A

(C) if the two quantities are equal

(D) if the relationship cannot be determined using the given information

Note: There are only four choices: do not choose (E). Consider the information centered above the quantities when deciding upon your choice. A variable or symbol that appears in a question means the same thing in Column A as in Column B and/or the centered information.

39.   **Column A**   **Column B**

$$\frac{10 - 2}{10 + 10} \qquad \frac{3}{4}$$

40.   **Column A**   **Column B**

Water flows through each of four pipes at a rate of 10 liters every half hour.

The total number of liters of water that   560 flow out of the 4 pipes in 7 hours

41.   **Column A**   **Column B**

The height h, in feet, of an object dropped from a height of 400 feet above the ground is given by $h = 400 - 16t^2$, where t is the time in seconds from when the object is dropped, and $0 \le t \le 5$.

The height of the object above the   180 ground, in feet, after $\frac{7}{2}$ seconds

42.   **Column A**   **Column B**

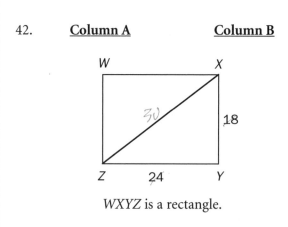

WXYZ is a rectangle.

The perimeter of   70 triangle *XYZ*

43.   **Column A**   **Column B**

$$3a + b = 4$$
$$5a + b = 12$$

a 3

44. **Column A**   **Column B**

$\dfrac{12}{1.24}$ 10

45. **Column A**   **Column B**

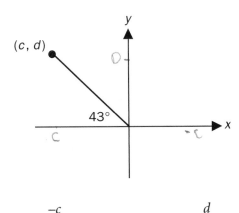

$-c$ d

46. **Column A**   **Column B**

$y \neq 0$

$-3y$ $5y$

47. **Column A**   **Column B**

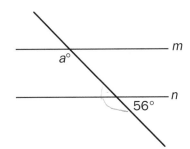

Line *m* is <u>not</u> parallel to line *n*.

$a - 56$ 68

48. **Column A**   **Column B**

g and *h* are consecutive multiples of 4.

$5(g - h)^2$ 80

49. **Column A**   **Column B**

Points *X*, *Y*, and *Z* are all on a straight line. The distance from point *X* to point *Z* is twice the distance from point *Y* to point *Z*.

The distance from point *X* to point *Y*   The distance from point *X* to point *Z*

50. **Column A**   **Column B**

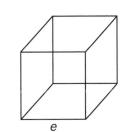 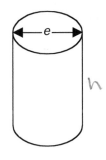

The volume of a cube with an edge of length *e* is equal to the volume of a right circular cylinder whose base has a diameter of length *e*.

The height of the right circular cylinder $\dfrac{4}{3}e$

51.
	Column A	**Column B**
	$\dfrac{1}{8^k} + \dfrac{1}{8^k} + \dfrac{1}{8^k}$	$\dfrac{1}{4^k}$

52.
	Column A	**Column B**

$$a^2 b < 0$$
$$b^3 c > 0$$

	Column A	**Column B**
	bc	0

$a = pos$
$c = neg$
$b = neg)$

53.
	Column A	**Column B**

$$x = 3^7 \times 5^8 \times 7^{12}$$

m is a positive integer.
35^m is a factor of x.

	Column A	**Column B**
	The greatest possible value of m	10

Directions for Questions 54–68: Select the best of the five answer choices given.

54. When 6 is reduced by $12x$, the result is equal to 14 multiplied by the sum of $5x$ and 8. The value of x can be found from which of the following equations?

(A) $12x - 6 = 14(5x + 8)$

(B) $12x + 6 = 14(5x) + 8$

(C) $6 - 12x = 14(5x - 8)$

(D) $6 - 12x = 14(5x + 8)$

(E) $6 - 12x = 14(5x) - 8$

55. What percent of 60 is 24?

(A) 24%

(B) 30%

(C) 40%

(D) 42%

(E) 52%

56. The expression $\dfrac{5^3}{\left(\dfrac{5^2}{5^7}\right)}$ is equivalent to which of the following?

(A) 5^8

(B) 5^4

(C) $\dfrac{1}{5^3}$

(D) $\dfrac{1}{5^4}$

(E) $\dfrac{1}{5^8}$

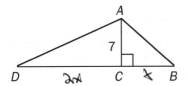

57. The area of triangle ABD in the figure above is 84 and the length of CD is twice the length of BC. What is the length of BC?

(A) 5

(B) 5.5

(C) 6

(D) 7

(E) 8

58. Every student in a room is either a freshman, a sophomore, a junior, or a senior. The ratio of freshmen to sophomores to juniors to seniors is 10:4:8:3. If there are a total of 450 students in the room, how many more freshmen than seniors are there in the room?

(A) 54

(B) 108

(C) 126

(D) 135

(E) 180

Questions 59-63 refer to the following graph.

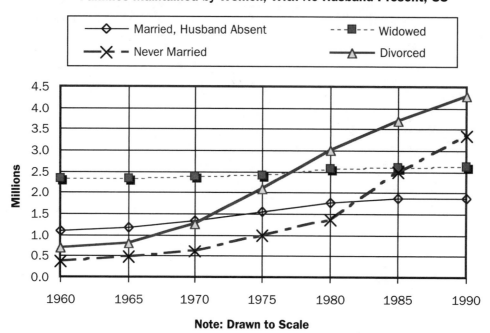

Families Maintained by Women, With No Husband Present, US

Note: Drawn to Scale

59. By approximately how many million did the number of families in the US maintained by a divorced female increase from 1960 to 1990?

(A) 0.2

(B) 0.8

(C) 3.0

(D) 3.7

(E) 4.5

60. In 1980 the population of families in the US maintained by widowed females was what fraction of the population of families in the US maintained by divorced females?

(A) $\dfrac{7}{15}$

(B) $\dfrac{17}{30}$

(C) $\dfrac{17}{20}$

(D) $\dfrac{29}{30}$

(E) $\dfrac{15}{13}$

61. What was the approximate percent increase in the number of families in the US maintained by married women with absent husbands from 1970 to 1980?

    (A) 5%

    (B) 33%

    (C) 73%

    (D) 200%

    (E) 225%

62. During which of the following periods was the increase in the number of families in the US maintained by a divorced woman closest to one million?

    (A) 1965 to 1970

    (B) 1970 to 1975

    (C) 1975 to 1980

    (D) 1980 to 1985

    (E) 1985 to 1990

63. The ratio of the number of families in the US maintained by a widowed female to the number of families in the US maintained by a married female with an absent husband was highest in which of the following years?

    (A) 1960

    (B) 1965

    (C) 1970

    (D) 1975

    (E) 1980

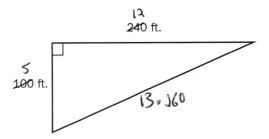

64. The figure above shows the fence surrounding a triangular garden. If the fence weighs 3 pounds per 5 feet, then what is the total weight of the fence, in pounds?

    (A) 240

    (B) 360

    (C) 480

    (D) 540

    (E) 1,000

65. Which of the following is equivalent to $y > 2y^2$?

    (A) $0 < y < \dfrac{1}{2}$

    (B) $y < \dfrac{1}{2}$

    (C) $y < 0$

    (D) $y > 0$

    (E) $y > \dfrac{1}{2}$

66. What is the value of $a + b$ in the figure above?

    (A) 31

    (B) 37

    (C) 43

    (D) 47

    (E) 53

67. The positive integers that are less than or equal to 420 and multiples of both 14 and 35 is what fraction of the positive integers that are less than 420 and multiples of 14?

    (A) $\dfrac{1}{28}$

    (B) $\dfrac{1}{14}$

    (C) $\dfrac{1}{10}$

    (D) $\dfrac{1}{7}$

    (E) $\dfrac{1}{5}$

68. The integer y is such that $14 < y^2 < 108$. What is the result of subtracting the smallest possible value of y from the greatest possible value of y?

    (A) 10

    (B) 12

    (C) 14

    (D) 20

    (E) 24

CHAPTER TWO

Diagnostic Test
Answers and Explanations

ANSWER KEY

Section 1: Analytical Writing

See Answers and Explanations section on page 31 for AWA scoring information.

Section 2: Verbal

1. B	16. E	31. E
2. C	17. D	32. D
3. A	18. D	33. D
4. C	19. A	34. C
5. B	20. B	35. A
6. B	21. C	36. B
7. B	22. D	37. E
8. D	23. A	38. B
9. C	24. C	
10. E	25. E	
11. D	26. A	
12. E	27. A	
13. C	28. B	
14. B	29. D	
15. D	30. A	

Section 3: Quantitative

39. B	54. D
40. C	55. C
41. A	56. A
42. A	57. E
43. A	58. C
44. B	59. D
45. A	60. C
46. D	61. B
47. D	62. C
48. C	63. A
49. D	64. B
50. B	65. A
51. D	66. C
52. A	67. E
53. B	68. D

ANSWERS AND EXPLANATIONS

Section 1: Analytical Writing

For both essays in the AWA, you will be evaluated on how well you:

- organize, develop, and express your ideas about the issue presented
- provide relevant supporting reasons and examples
- control the elements of standard written English

For the Issue essay, you must analyze the issue and explain your views. There is no correct answer. For the Argument essay, you must critique the argument presented. You are *not* being asked to present your own views on the subject.

The AWA score is an average of the scores given for the two essays. Scores range from 0 to 6 (best). Each essay is given two, independent ratings, one of which may be performed by an electronic system that evaluates more than 50 structural and linguistic features, including organization of ideas, syntactic variety, and topical analysis. If the two ratings differ by more than one point, an additional evaluation will be made.

The following table will give you a general idea of the guidelines a GRE grader will have in mind when reading your essays:

6: Outstanding Essay

- Insightfully presents and convincingly supports an opinion on the issue or a critique of the argument
- Ideas are very clear, well organized, and logically connected
- Shows superior control of language: grammar, stylistic variety, and accepted conventions of writing; minor flaws may occur

5: Strong Essay

- Presents and strongly supports an opinion on the issue or a critique of the argument
- Ideas are generally clear and well organized; connections are logical
- Shows solid control of language: grammar, stylistic variety, and accepted conventions of writing; minor flaws may occur

4: Adequate Essay

- Presents and adequately supports an opinion on the issue or a critique of the argument
- Ideas are fairly clear and adequately organized; logical connections are satisfactory
- Shows satisfactory control of language: grammar, stylistic variety, and accepted conventions of writing; some flaws may occur

3: Limited Essay

- Succeeds only partially in presenting and supporting an opinion on the issue or a critique of the argument
- Ideas may be unclear and poorly organized
- Shows less than satisfactory control of language: contains significant mistakes in grammar, usage, and sentence structure

2: Seriously Flawed Essay

- Shows little success in presenting and supporting an opinion on the issue or a critique of the argument
- Ideas lack organization
- Meaning is impeded by many serious mistakes in grammar, usage, and sentence structure

1: Fundamentally Deficient Essay

- Fails to present a coherent opinion on the issue or a critique of the argument
- Ideas are seriously disorganized
- Lacks meaning due to widespread severe mistakes in grammar, usage, and sentence structure

0: Unscorable Essay

- Essay completely ignores topic

Following are two sample essays in response to the AWA assignments. Both essays would earn a perfect score.

KAPLAN

Sample Issue Essay (Score 6)

Present your perspective on the issue below, using relevant reasons and/or examples to support your views.

> "Every e-mail originating from an unknown user may contain a virus. Companies should maintain active vigilance to prevent employees from opening e-mails that are from unknown users."

These days, it is well known that computer viruses are often transmitted from one computer to another via email. On the surface, it would seem that a company could control the spread of viruses to its computers by instructing employees not to open emails from strangers. However, this solution does not allow for the complex ways that viruses spread, and in addition may restrict the ability of some employees to do their jobs effectively.

One way that computer viruses spread in the workplace is when an employee mistakenly opens a suspect email from a stranger. Certainly, this should be discouraged. Employees should be instructed to use common sense in deciding which emails to open and should be encouraged to delete emails from obviously bogus addresses or with dubious subject lines. However, viruses are also spread in many other, less obvious ways. Sophisticated viruses and worms, for instance, can send themselves via email to everyone in a person's email address book. In this case, the virus would be coming from someone the employee might know very well. This type of virus could easily slip through the cracks if the only criterion for identifying suspicious emails is that they come from unknown users. Still other viruses may enter a computer via a connection to the Internet without any action at all from its user and are virtually invisible to anyone but an experienced code interpreter. In this case, attention to incoming email is beside the point.

In addition, some types of employees must open emails from strangers in order to do their jobs. Many customer service and support functions are now being handled by email, especially in the technology sector. These employees do not have the luxury of choosing which emails to open: the majority of their emails come from unknown users needing help. If a company were unwise enough to restrict access to these emails, they would soon find they had created a number of unhappy customers, which is never good for business. Inquiries regarding public relations and potential clients are also examples of types of emails from unknown users that most companies would like have their employees receive.

A company would also be remiss in assuming it could completely control the behavior of its employees. We are all susceptible to occasional lapses in judgment, and everyone makes mistakes. It is not fair to place the burden of virus control on the shoulders of the average employee. Instead, companies should rely on experts in the field to create systems for preventing viruses that do not rely on a judgment call by someone without the experience to make it. Companies must indeed stay vigilant, but not towards whether or not their employees are opening the wrong emails. Companies must instead stay vigilant to the ever-changing world of computer virus creation and prevention by engaging the services of expert professionals who will do a much better job of protecting them from a debilitating virus than an employee whose expertise lies in accounting, sales, or any of the other areas necessary to run a given business.

Therefore, simple attention to preventing employees from opening certain types of emails is not an effective strategy in preventing the spread of viruses in light of the many different advanced methods currently being used in delivering devastating viruses to the systems of the world's businesses. Companies that want to prevent themselves from being affected by increasingly insidious computer viruses should adopt a more comprehensive and technologically savvy approach.

Sample Argument Essay (Score 6)

Discuss how well reasoned you find this argument.

The following appeared in a letter to the editor of a local newspaper:

"Television cartoons portray an unrealistic image of violence. All too often, one cartoon character uses dangerous implements to inflict bodily harm on another, and the effects of this violence upon the other character are completely negligible. If our children were to imitate this behavior, it would be catastrophic. Therefore, all cartoons should revolve around non-violent conflicts, and all violent children's programming should be banned from the networks."

The premise that all television cartoons containing violence should be banned because of the possible negative effects they have on children is flawed. On the surface, the idea of banning violent content directed at children may seem to be in the best interest of creating a less violent society, but the author of this letter fails to present any evidence that children are prompted to violent behavior by watching cartoons on television. Instead, the author suggests an extreme solution, the censorship of the medium, to a problem that may not even exist.

The main failure in the author's argument stems from his reliance on supposition. Even if we accept the idea that cartoons are too violent and something should be done, by saying "if our children were to imitate this behavior, it would be catastrophic," the author essentially acknowledges that he had not shown sufficient evidence to support his claim. Cartoons such as Roadrunner and Tom and Jerry have used unrealistic displays of violence for many years, plenty of time for any correlation between children's watching these kinds of shows and their subsequent behavior to be adequately studied. However, the author of this letter does not refer to any such evidence to support his argument. In fact, the author could have presented evidence from his own experience observing children, but he does not do this either. The letter is wholly concerned with the author's opinion without any proof of a link existing in the first place.

Even if the author was able to back up his claim that extremely bad conduct amongst animated characters on television causes similar behavior in children, the solution he proposes is not a reasonable one. Recent innovations in television ratings systems, used in conjunction with technology such as the "V" chip, allow parents to have control over the programs their children watch. This approach, rather than the draconian one the author suggests, is more appropriate for a democratic society. Particularly in a free market, supply is governed by demand. If parents deem that certain shows do not constitute suitable entertainment for their children, those shows will soon disappear from the marketplace.

We would all like to find solutions to the growing violence in our culture. Children should certainly be taught that their actions have consequences, but no evidence is presented here that violence in cartoons creates a climate where young people think that violence is acceptable. Even if the letter presented concrete evidence of this phenomenon, outright censorship is rarely a solution to a complex problem such as this.

Section 2: Verbal

1. B

This sentence begins with a description of an observed change in the park's natural hot springs. The key word "because" indicates that its following phrase will give a reason for the change. At the end of the sentence, we learn that "human disruption" is the reason. The blank, then, contains a word that describes what happens to a balance when it is disrupted. Choice (A), *understood*, is not supported by the context. Choice (B), *unstable*, squares very well with the notion of a disrupted balance, and is the credited answer. Choice (C), *observed*, like choice (A), does not reflect the disruption mentioned in the sentence. Choice (D), *contaminated*, has the right word charge; but, since the disruption was not due to the hot springs themselves, which can be contaminated by humans, but to the ecological balance of the hot springs, which cannot logically be contaminated, choice (D) must be discarded. Choice (E), *accelerated*, doesn't make much sense here.

2. C

A novelist wrote eloquently about a place and time that he did not experience firsthand: that's unexpected. At first glance, choice (A) *doubtful* seems like a possibility; however, the fact that the novelist did in fact publish such an eloquent book dispels any doubt that the writer's origins might have engendered. Choice (B), *natural*, is the opposite of our prediction. Choice (C), *surprising*, works perfectly in the sentence's context and is therefore the credited answer. Neither choice (D), *worrying*, nor choice (E), *laughable*, is related to the context here.

3. A

In this sentence, physics is being compared to economics. The word "like" indicates that the two share something: the maintenance of something through similarly complex balances of actions and reactions. We know, then, that the correct answer will have something to do with balances. We can also narrow down the search by looking for ideas or concepts that both physics and economics share, and eliminating any answers that are unique to just one of the fields. Choice (A), *equilibrium*, refers to a state of balance, and therefore is a perfect match for our prediction. Choice (B), *goods*, pertains strictly to economics; it is a term describing things that we value. It doesn't have any relation to physics, which is the study of interaction among matter. The reverse is true of choice (C), *inertia*, a physics term which pertains to individual objects rather than balances. Choice (D), *benefits*, isn't related to balances. Like choice (B), choice (E), *value*, is an economics concept. The correct answer here has to relate to each science.

4. C

The first clause of this two-blank sentence states a fact about us: we have increasingly come to feel or think a certain way about corporal punishment, which is the infliction of non-lethal bodily injury as punishment for crimes. The semicolon indicates that the following statement will continue the thought of the preceding statement. In the statement following the semicolon, we find that we don't believe that corporal punishment is an effective way to prevent crime. The correct answer choice, then, should reflect our disbelief in the efficacy of corporal punishment as a deterrent. Choice (A) doesn't do that; in fact, we know it's wrong because the first blank, *convinced of*, contradicts the second part of the sentence, which states that we aren't convinced. Regarding choice (B), while this practice may well be *dehumanizing* for the people who are punished, the sentence is concerned with our, rather than their, responses. Choice (C) works; we are *skeptical of*, or uncertain of, the *deterrent* effects of corporal punishment, since we're no longer convinced that such punishment actually deters anyone. According to (D), we are increasingly *reliant upon* the *political* effect of corporal punishment, when in fact the sentence states that we no longer believe that it is effective. Choice (E) is also wrong, as we certainly aren't feeling *empowered*, and the sentence doesn't suggest anything about corporal punishment being *strengthening*.

5. B

The first part of the sentence up to the semicolon suggests that disagreement over the appropriate use of force has been a constant issue in international relations that has recurred over time. The keyword "therefore," which begins the second part of the sentence, indicates that the second part will be the conclusion drawn from the first. Choice (A), *spurious*, implies that current international disputes are false or illegitimate; the first part of the sentence suggests only that such disagreements have happened, not whether they were legitimate or not. Choice (B), *unique*, fills the bill much better: if disagreements occur consistently, then it is presumptuous to suggest that they are *unique*. Choice (C), *relevant*, doesn't work; the first part of the sentence doesn't say anything about the relevance of the disagreements. If anything, the fact that disputes occur repeatedly indicates that they are *relevant*, which makes (C) completely wrong. Choice (D), *perennial*, is a trap answer; the first part of the sentence states that disagreement over the appropriate use of force is in fact a consistent, or *perennial*, issue, but the second part states that it would be presumptuous to think that that is the case. Similarly, choice (E), *irresolvable*, makes a statement about disagreements that isn't supported by the sentence.

6. B

The opening of this two-blank sentence says something about how we behave in heated arguments. The presence of the keyword "with" indicates that the phrase following "with" will describe this behavior further, perhaps by relating an identifying trait. The word "rather" in this phrase introduced by "with" indicates as well that we should be looking for answers for the second blank that indicate the primacy of feelings over facts, and, by extension, emotion over logic. Choice (A) doesn't give us the right answer for the second blank; our prediction is for an answer that indicates the primacy of feelings over facts, rather than the other way around. Moreover, the answer for the first blank is too extreme; there isn't any implication that emotion is *destroying* logic, just that it's overpowering it. Choice (B)'s suggestion for the first blank, *trump*, meaning to surpass or beat, has the proper magnitude for the context; the second suggestion, *appealing to*, works as well. We'll hold on to this one as we check the remaining possibilities. Choice (C) doesn't give us the correct answer for the first blank; the sentence suggests that emotion and logic are in opposition, not that one *empowers* the other. Choice (D) is something of a trap. One could argue that emotion *displays* a logic of its own, and that both parties *refer to* feelings rather than facts. However, the sentence constructed by using (D)'s choices is too loose to be correct here, especially when compared with (B). Choice (E) is wrong as well; emotion and logic aren't *equal*, as far as this sentence is concerned.

7. B

The author explains that Greek tragedies were popular because they allowed audiences to think about something in relation to something else. Our principle clue is in the middle clause: the phrase "against one another" indicates that the answer will have to do with human, not human-divine, interactions. Choice (A) focuses on the audiences' relationships to their gods. As we have already noted, the primary issue here is the audience members' relationships to each other. Choice (B) suggests that, as a result of seeing the tragedies, audiences had opportunities to consider their *duties* to their *compatriots*, or fellow citizens; had the characters in the tragedies been so thoughtful they might have avoided both committing their crimes and receiving their punishments. Regarding choice (C), while in some cases the crimes in question may have concerned *allegiance* to *communities*, this relationship isn't part of the middle clause, and thus this can't be the answer. The same is true of choice (D). Choice (E), the trap, suggests that the tragedies were ways of showing audiences the power of their *governments* to enforce laws and the repercussions the audiences might expect for *opposition* to those governments. Since *governments* aren't mentioned in the sentence, choice (E) can't be right.

8. D

An ASCETIC chooses to live in an AUSTERE way. Which of the following pairs is joined by the same bridge? Choice (A) offers *adolescent*, a person who is not yet *mature*. A *rustic*, a person who lives in a rural area, does not necessarily live a *spartan* lifestyle. *Disciple* and *reverent* in choice (C) do not have a strong and necessary relationship. Choice (D) presents *warrior*, an individual who has chosen to live a *martial*, or warlike, life. This is a strong match with our prediction. Choice (E)'s *zealot* has *fervent* beliefs, but this is not the relationship we seek.

9. C

Our initial bridge might be: a SURGEON uses a SCALPEL. A quick survey of the answer choices, however, indicates that we'll need a more specific bridge, since several of the answers match tools with the professionals who use them. To make the bridge more specific, we can ask, "a SURGEON uses a SCALPEL to do what?" We know that a SCALPEL is a cutting tool, so we can adjust our bridge to: a SURGEON uses a SCALPEL to cut. Now let's look at the answers. Choice (A) is a classic trap; while a *soldier* may use a *bayonet* to cut, the order of the words is the reverse of that of the stem pair. Choice (B)'s *anvil* isn't a cutting tool, so we can eliminate it. Choice (C) sounds right: a *gardener* uses *shears* to cut. In order to be sure, though, let's check the other two answers. Choice (D) doesn't work: a *wrench* isn't a cutting tool. Choice (E) is wrong for the same reason.

10. E

A PROLOGUE is the beginning component of a NOVEL. Choices (A) and (B) can both be eliminated because neither pair have that bridge. A *scene* is not specifically the beginning of a *play*, so we can eliminate choice (C). In choice (D), a *seal* is made in *wax*, but is not the beginning component of *wax*. Eliminate. However, Choice (E)'s pair of *overture* and *opera* match our prediction perfectly.

11. D

To AMBLE is to WALK without direction. Choice (A) presents *look* and *stare*; to *stare* is to *look* intently in one direction. Choice (B) doesn't fit; *frown* and *scowl* are synonyms. Choice (C) is a trap answer. To *tack* is to *sail* in a zig-zag pattern, which certainly isn't the same things as without direction, so this choice isn't right. Choice (D) works: to *wander* is to *travel* without direction. To be certain, let's check the last possibility. Choice (E)'s *speak* does not mean to *yell* without direction.

12. E

An ACORN is the seed-bearing part (or fruit) of an OAK tree. Let's compare this bridge to our answer choices. Choice (A) seems to reverse the bridge, but, since a *needle*, in fact, is a leaf not the fruit of a *pine*, the analogy is not comparable at all. If our bridge were an ACORN grows on an OAK, choice (B) might be a contender, because *ivy* often grows on *walls*. But that's not our bridge. Choice (C) can be eliminated by the same reasoning we used to eliminate (B). An *almond* is a type of *nut*, but this is not the relationship we're looking for. Eliminate (D). Finally, a *grape* is the seed-bearing part—the fruit—of the *vine*; thus, choice (E) is the credited answer.

13. C

A classic bridge: one thing is a greater degree of another. In this case, to ENRAPTURE is a much stronger word than PLEASE; we might say to ENRAPTURE is to PLEASE a great deal. We need a pair in which the second term is a greater degree of the first. The two words in choice (A) not only do not match the stem pair's bridge, but they also have barely any relationship at all. Choice (B)'s *ebb* and *wane* are synonyms; one is not a greater degree than another. Choice (C) has the bridge we want: to *beguile* is to *charm* a great deal. Choice (D) offers *appear* and *resolve*. A secondary definition for *resolve* is "to render part of something visible and distinct," which makes *resolve* a word that is a lesser, rather than a greater, degree of *appear*. Choice (E)'s *bemoan* means to express *regret*, but the first word is not a greater degree of the second.

14. B

To COUNTERMAND means to cancel or reverse, particularly with regard to an ORDER. Choice (A) won't work with that bridge; to *delay* isn't to cancel a *conference*. Choice (B), however, will work: to *revoke* is to cancel *permission*. In order to be certain, however, let's go through the other choices. To *deviate* is to change, but not necessarily to cancel, *course*; the specificity of our bridge pays off here. If we insert choice (D)'s suggestions into our bridge, we get to *retire* is to cancel *debt*, which sounds promising. But *retire* in this context means satisfy or pay off, rather than cancel or reverse, so choice (D) won't work. Choice (E)'s *elevate* does not mean to cancel a *position*, but rather to raise it or make it more powerful.

15. D

MASTICATE means " to grind (food) with the TEETH." TEETH are used to MASTICATE food. What pair has the same bridge? While *feet* are used to *leap*, our bridge contains a noun (TEETH) acting on another noun (food). Look for a better match. Choice (B) tries to trick us since it has to do with eating, but the bridge is not correct.

File is an action one does to his or her *nails*. A *millstone* is used to *grind* grains. This looks like a good match. Finally, someone *cracks* a *chestnut*; therefore, choice (E) is wrong. Choice (D) is the best answer.

16. E

A LIMERICK is a form of POETRY that is viewed with some ambivalence; some think it clever, others consider it foolery. We want our answer to have a similar sort of negative relationship. Choice (A) doesn't work in our bridge; *radio* and *television* are different media. Likewise, choice (B)'s *conspiracy* isn't necessarily a subset of *ruse*, which means trick or pretense, so this choice isn't correct either. Choice (C) offers *farce* and *satire*; both are types of comedy, but one is not a type of the other, so this choice won't do. Choice (D) presents *midway*, which is a part of a *fair*, but because there isn't anything ambivalent about a *midway*, this isn't a perfect fit for our prediction. Choice (E) offers *caricature* and *portraiture*. A *caricature* is a picture deliberately making use of ridiculous exaggeration or distortion that is a type of *portraiture*, although this is an ambiguous definition: some *caricature* is regarded as high, some argue that *caricature* is simply an entertainment or cartoon. Because this relationship fits our bridge and has the negative flavor of the stem pair, choice (E) is the best answer.

Passage Analysis:

Topic: Intelligence Testing

Scope: The usefulness of intelligence testing

Purpose: To review the limitations and benefits of intelligence testing, while favoring the benefits

Paragraph 1: A review of the limitations and flaws of intelligence testing

Paragraph 2: The benefits of intelligence testing. Although objectively presenting both sides of the testing controversy, the author lobbies that the merits of testing outweigh the drawbacks.

17. D

Paragraph 1 references the controversy over intelligence testing and focuses on the arguments of testing opponents. Paragraph 2 cites evidence in favor of testing and the author's conclusion that intelligence testing is essential. Choice (B) is tempting because the passage does discuss two competing schools of thought. However, this is a half-right/half-wrong trap since the author advocates testing in paragraph 2, never attempting to unify the competing points of view. Despite the imposing language in choices (A), (C), and (E), these are all off target. At no time does the passage discuss a phenomenon, hypothesis, or paradox.

18. D

The author's purpose in mentioning hearing, vision, and speech problems is two-fold. He or she both wants to illustrate the multitude of dimensions that may affect IQ scores as well as to provide a concrete example of poor test interpretation. Statement III is incorrect because the author does not mention labeling or psychological damage.

19. A

The author says that opponents of testing feel the tests fail to assess social abilities or practical skills required for daily life. The word "never" is a tip off that choice (B) is too extreme to be correct. Opponents of testing feel the tests are flawed—not that they should never be used. Choice (C) distorts the author's wording. Opponents of testing are concerned that creative answers may not receive deserved points because they are not in the standardized scoring guide. We can infer that opponents of testing feel these answers should receive points—but not necessarily that they should receive *more* points. Choice (D) is outside the scope of the question. Choice (E) is again too extreme. Although the passage states that test administrators must be qualified, there is no suggestion that "most" administrators are unreliable.

20. B

This is a *global* question seeking the overall purpose of the passage. In our roadmap, the purpose reads, "Although objectively presenting both sides of the testing controversy, the author lobbies that the merits of testing outweigh the drawbacks." Therefore, the correct answer will mention both the positive and negative aspects of IQ testing. Choices (A) and (D) can immediately be eliminated because they both imply discussion of only the negative aspects of IQ testing: poor test administrators in choice (A) and an attack on the criteria of testing in choice (D) (the word "attack" here implies that fault will be found only with the criteria, which is certainly not the case). Choice (C) can also be eliminated, because, although an explanation of the administration of IQ tests sounds neutral, only the flaws of the system are actually mentioned in the answer. In fact, the passage never explains the administration of the test, although the first paragraph does imply that opponents of IQ testing think that there are flaws. Only choices (B) and (E) imply a presentation of both positive and negative aspects of IQ testing, but choice (E) is much too strong. As our roadmap says, the passage presents both sides of the testing controversy "objectively"—that is, without contradicting either side. In fact, the passage acknowledges the potential drawbacks (or what the opponents would see as "sources of inaccuracy"), but argues that IQ testing is valid (efficacious or useful) despite them.

21. C

This is a *detail* question with a slight twist: you're asked for something that the author does not mention, instead of something the author does mention. There is the added difficulty that all of the answer choices appear in the passage in some form, which means that the correct answer will either be a distortion of something mentioned in the passage or in a different context from that mentioned in the question stem.

First, find the part of the passage that deals with the benefits of IQ testing. Since your roadmap will tell you paragraph 1 treats the views of the opponents to IQ testing, the benefits of IQ testing should appear in paragraph 2, which treats the arguments in favor of IQ testing. Of the answer choices, only choice (C) appears in paragraph 1 as part of the final sentence. Comparison between this sentence and the wording of choice (C) shows that the answer distorts the language of the passage. The sentence says that "poor test administrators may mistake a hearing, speech, or vision impediment" for a sign of low IQ The answer says the opposite of what the author says.

22. D

Here is an *inference* question asking you to find the assumption underlying a specific statement in the passage. As the word inference implies, the assumption will not necessarily be stated outright, but may need to be drawn from the context. Let's look for the words "poor test administrators" in the passage. These words appear in the final sentence of paragraph 1, but at the end of a several sentence portion of the paragraph dealing with poor or unqualified test administrators in general. This section begins with the words "Lastly, because of the value placed on IQ scores, intelligence tests administered by unqualified or disinterested individuals…" and goes on to discuss various ways in which bad test administrators can cause harm, including an inability to recognize the effects of socioeconomic status, ethnicity, current health, and family circumstances on an individual's responses, or even to misdiagnose physical impediments to hearing, speech, or vision as signs of low IQ or mental retardation. What general assumption can we make about the effect test administrators can have on the results of a test? That test administrators have a significant effect on a test taker's results. Only choice (D) says this. Be very careful when reading the other answer choices because some of them use language that appears in the passage. Choice (A) mentions "disinterested" test administrators, but the passage does not state that many administrators are disinterested or that any attempt to sabotage results. Choice (B) is too extreme in suggesting that IQ tests are "nearly impossible to administer." Choice (C) is also too extreme with the word "never." Choice (E), although the word "biases" suggest the socioeconomic status, ethnicity, current health, and family circumstances that unqualified testers may fail to consider, the word "always" makes this choice also too extreme.

23. A

Here is an *inference* question based on the use of a specific phrase "test-taking sophistication" in its context. First, let's look at the context. Although "sophistication" is normally a positive attribute, the word's context may suggest otherwise. The passage states, "Although scores can serve as valuable indices of potential and ability, they may also reflect personal attitudes and test-taking sophistication." The word "although" contrasts the first clause with the second. Since "valuable indices of potential and ability" of the first clause must be positive, the "personal attitudes and test-taking sophistication" of the second must be negative—something that would hinder the effectiveness of a test of native intelligence. Now address the answer choices: which one of them would hinder the effectiveness of a test in native intelligence? Would a person's familiarity with the procedures of standardized testing independent of the specific content of the test hinder the effectiveness of a test of native intelligence? Yes. If a person can produce correct answers without actually knowing the content simply through familiarity with the type of test, then the test results will necessarily not reflect the test taker's knowledge of the topic, regardless of what the topic is. The other answers are all positive attributes that will either allow the test taker to access native intelligence easily, such as choices (B) and (C), or add to a person's native intelligence, such as choices (D) and (E). Choices (D) and (E) have the added trap that they both seem to refer to usual definitions of sophistication: either knowing a lot about art and literature through the advantages of wealth, choice (D); or having varied life experiences, choice (E).

Passage Analysis:

Topic: Latin and Greek writers

Scope: The relevance of Latin and Greek writers today

Purpose: To argue that Latin and Greek writers should be read to supplement the reading of recent authors

Paragraph 1: Latin and Greek writers are now seldom read; many argue that this is good because writers who reflect today's reality are more deserving; this is shortsighted

Paragraph 2: Supporters of this change don't argue that the texts are irrelevant; instead, they believe that recent texts are more important; students should read both ancient and current works; this is convincing

Paragraph 3: Knowledge of the classics remains essential; all Western literature explores variations on a few general themes; balance is needed; students should supplement recent authors with the ancients; readers will be surprised at the relevance of ancients

24. C

This is a *global* question. It tests your ability to find the *primary purpose* of the passage. The primary purpose of this passage is to argue that Latin and Greek writers should be read more often. Choice (C) is the correct answer, since the passage tells us that currently, these writers are hardly ever read. Therefore, to advocate that these authors be read, the author is arguing that the current curriculum must be changed. Choice (A) is the *opposite* of the right answer. The author is disagreeing with the common belief that these authors are not relevant. Choice (B) is also the *opposite* of the correct answer; the author would be likely to agree with a school of criticism that emphasizes these writers. An entire paragraph, the second, explains why Latin and Greek writers are out of favor, and, as such, why certain authors are read more often than others. However, this explanation (choice (D)) is not the primary concern of the passage as a whole. Choice (E) represents a *classic trap* that appears frequently on the GRE. It is too extreme. The author is not arguing that these authors need to be studied more than or instead of all others, only that it is a mistake to leave them out entirely.

25. E

The words *the passage suggests*, tells you that this is an *inference* question. The correct answer to an inference question is almost always a close paraphrase of something in the passage. In this case, the correct answer will paraphrase the author's opinion. Choice (E) does exactly that. Choice (A) is another example of an extreme answer choice. There is no indication that the author believes that *all* that is needed to study literature is these ancient authors. Choice (B) is another *opposite* answer. The author believes that studying these authors is important to understand later works. Choices (C) and (D) are outside the scope of the passage. There is no discussion of the study of the Latin and Greek languages, or any language for that matter.

26. A

In this paragraph, the first sentence serves to introduce the topic, which is an explanation of why some academics and scholars support the decentralization of classic texts. Thus, choice (A) is the correct answer. Choice (B) is tempting, as the author does believe that ancient writers are still important, and paragraph 2 does tell us that they are not read as often as they once were. However, the second paragraph does not attempt to prove that ancient authors are still important. Rather, paragraph 4 is where the author addresses this issue. Choice (C) is wrong because the second paragraph does not describe the author's own beliefs. (D) is half right and half wrong, in that the second paragraph explains a position that the author would like modified.

However, the author waits until the third paragraph to explain the flaw that he or she finds in the position. Choice (E), also tempting, echoes one of the author's major points, but it's not a point that the author makes in the second paragraph and is also too extreme.

27. A

This is an *inference* question and the correct answer is typically a close paraphrase of the passage. Only Choice (A) echoes the passage, paraphrasing a point the author makes in the third paragraph: "all western literature takes the form of permutations on a few general themes...explicated by Latin and Greek writers." Choice (B) is the *opposite* of the correct answer. The author tells us that they were "once central to a basic education." Choice (C) is both an extreme answer and also not likely to be in line with the author's opinion since it minimizes the importance of reading these ancient works. We know that the author believes that Latin and Greek authors are important to *all students* of literature. Choice (D) is also too extreme. The author is in no way asserting that these authors are superior to contemporary authors, only that it is necessary to read the ancient works to fully understand contemporary authors. Choice (E) uses extreme language to say the opposite of what the author says in the last sentence of the passage.

28. B

MANDATORY means "compulsory" or "obligatory," so the antonym must be something that has a meaning related to "not required." Choice (A), *daily*, implies that something happens regularly or in a pattern, which isn't what we want. Choice (B), *optional*, sounds like an excellent match for our prediction. Choice (C), *nugatory*, means "inoperative" or "useless." In this context, it is an oddball answer—a far more difficult word than the other answer choices—and therefore very likely wrong. Choices (D), *boring*, and (E), *calm*, also don't work.

29. D

LAMBASTE means "to censure verbally." Its negative word charge means we'll want an antonym that suggests praise or honor. Choice (A), *enervate*, means "to weaken," so it's not what we're looking for. Choice (B) is something of a trap. If we didn't know what LAMBASTE meant and tried to break it into its constituent parts, we'd see *-baste*, which might trigger us to choose *cook*. We know that choice (B) won't work, however, for the simple reason that *cook* has no good antonym, and any choice that lacks a clear antonym can be ignored. Choice (C), *censure*, is closer to being a synonym for the stem word than it is to being an antonym. Choice (D), *praise*, fits our prediction perfectly, and carries the requisite positive word charge. Lastly, there isn't a good one-word antonym for choice (E)'s *discuss*.

30. A

OSCILLATE means "waver" or "swing back and forth." If we were unsure of its definition, the sound might remind us of the word "vacillate," which means "to hesitate" or "waver." Choice (A), *remain constant*, matches our prediction well. Since choices (B), *move quickly*, and (C), *turn slowly*, suggest movement at opposite speeds, we could eliminate both of them even without our prediction because they're close to being antonyms of each other. Choice (D), *look around*, and choice (E), *speak quietly*, won't work because we recall from our prediction that the correct answer will specifically concern lack of movement.

31. E

RANCOR means "deep-seated ill will." We can predict, then, that an antonym for the stem word means something like "positive feelings" or "friendship." Choice (A)'s *neutrality* suggests feelings that are neither positive nor negative. Choice (B), *bellicosity*, or warlike condition, and choice (C), *peacefulness*, are opposites of one another, and as such can't be the correct answers. We can eliminate choice (D), *trepidation*, on the basis of its negative word charge. (RANCOR is a strongly negative word, and the correct answer will be strongly positive.) Choice (E)'s *friendship* is a strong match for our prediction, and therefore is the credited answer.

32. D

Someone who is SUPPLIANT must beg for assistance. A related but more common word is supplicant, or beggar. Which of the choices has a meaning that is the opposite of this? Choice (A) has only a loose connection to the stem word, and in any case *forgiving* is more similar than opposite in meaning to it. The stem word doesn't really have anything to do with appropriateness in choice (B). We could immediately eliminate choice (C), *starving*, because it has the same word charge—negative and in need—as SUPPLIANT. Choice (D) works well: the opposite of needing to beg for assistance is not to need assistance at all—being *self-sufficient*. Beware, though, of choice (E), the trap. If we didn't know what SUPPLIANT meant and began casting about for words with similar-sounding roots, we might come across the word *supple*, which means pliant. And *inflexible* is an excellent antonym for that word.

33. D

DEBASE means "to lower in character, esteem or quality." If we weren't sure of its meaning, we might recognize the word root *de-*, which we've seen in other words to indicate downward motion. Armed with this clue, we would then look for an antonym among the choices that suggests raising up. We might also use word charge here; DEBASE is a strongly negative word, so the correct answer will have a strongly positive charge. Choice (A), *alleviate*, means "to make bad conditions better." Although this choice has the necessary connotation of upward movement, conditions are not related to the meaning of the stem word. Choice (B), *embark*, meaning "to leave on a trip," is a trap that plays on an alternate meaning of the word root *de-*. Choice (C), *evaluate*, does not indicate motion in any direction; moreover, like (B) it has no word charge. Choice (D), *honor*, means "to give glory or recognition," which, with its good match for our prediction and strongly positive word charge, sounds like the right answer. Choice (E), *cheapen*, is closer to being a synonym of the stem word than it is an antonym.

34. C

PENURY means "an oppressive lack of resources." We are looking for a choice that describes the opposite of a lack of resources: wealth or plenty. Simply knowing the charge of the stem word—strongly negative—enables us to winnow out any choices that aren't strongly positive. Choice (A), *righteousness*, is only loosely related to the stem word. Choice (B), *fastidiousness*, or "meticulous attention to detail," doesn't work either. Choice (C), *affluence*, matches our prediction well and is the correct answer. While choice (D), *charm*, has a positive word charge, its meaning does not match our prediction. Choice (E), *boldness*, is an unrelated concept.

35. A

ABROGATE means "to abolish or annul." As a clue, we might recall instances in which we've heard the stem word used: "The U.S. ABROGATED a treaty with Russia," meaning that the U.S. annulled an agreement it made. Therefore, we should look for answers that indicate living up to an agreement. We should also note that ABROGATE has a fairly strong negative word charge. Choice (A)'s *ratify*, which means "to approve and give formal sanction to," looks like an excellent match for our prediction. Choice (B) doesn't work; to *espouse* means "to take up and support," and has too loose a connection to the stem word to be correct. Choice (C), *compromise*, also doesn't fit. Choice (D), *annul*, is the definition of the stem, and therefore cannot be correct. Choice (E), *question*, is unrelated to the stem word.

36. B

None of the choices is a verb, so we need to come up with a secondary meaning for BECOMING. As an adjective, BECOMING means "appropriate or suitable," so we need an antonym that suggests "inappropriate or unsuitable." We should also note that BECOMING has a positive word charge, and that consequently the correct answer will have one that is negative. Choice (A), *vainglorious*, which means "boastful" or "characterized by or exhibiting excessive vanity," has a negative charge, but its meaning is not opposite that of the stem word. Choice (B), *unseemly*, works; it has a negative charge and also signifies inappropriateness. Choice (C)'s suggestion *decorous*, or proper, is too close in meaning and charge to the stem word to be an antonym. For similar reasons, choice (D)'s *carefully composed* does not work. Choice (E)'s *readily available* is unrelated to the stem word here.

37. E

A CODA is a conclusion or closing part of a statement or musical work. Its antonym will be concerned with beginnings. Choice (A)'s *footnote* can occur anywhere in a piece of work, as can a *refrain* in choice (D). Choice (B), *epilogue*, is quite close in meaning to the stem word; we might deduce this if we recall that the word root *epi-* means "after" (that is "added to") or "upon." An *apostrophe* in choice (C) is a direct address to an absent person or idea that can happen anywhere in a piece. The use of *apostrophe* employs the secondary meaning of this common word, which makes it something of a trap. Choice (E), *preamble*, fits the bill nicely, and is the credited answer. We could arrive at this conclusion even if we didn't know what a *preamble* was by noting the word root *pre-*, meaning before.

38. B

The stem word means "revealing" or "marked by a smug, ingratiating, or false earnestness." But even if we don't recall the precise definition of SMARMY, we may very well know its strongly negative word charge, on which basis alone we could eliminate choice (A), *lascivious*, and choice (E), *smug*, both of which are negative as well. Choice (B), *earnest*, with its strongly positive word charge, looks like a strong candidate, but we'll check the remaining answers just to be sure. Choice (C) is a trap answer; it doesn't have anything to do with either the stem word or the other choices, but it may confuse us if we have an imperfect definition of SMARMY, such as "unclean" or "ill-kempt," in mind. Choice (D), *erudite* has fairly neutral word charge and a meaning unrelated to that of the stem word.

Section 3: Quantitative

39. B

Simplify Column A. $\frac{10-2}{10+10} = \frac{8}{20} = \frac{2}{5}$, which is less than $\frac{3}{4}$.

40. C

Each pipe has a flow of 10 liters every 30 minutes, or $\frac{1}{2}$ hour. So each pipe has a

flow of $\dfrac{10}{\left(\frac{1}{2}\right)} = 10 \times \frac{2}{1} = 20$ liters per hour.

In 7 hours, one pipe will have $20 \times 7 = 140$ liters flow out. Then in 7 hours, 4 pipes will have $140 \times 4 = 560$ liters of water flow out.

41. A

To find the height when $t = \frac{7}{2}$, let's substitute $\frac{7}{2}$ for t in $h = 400 - 16t^2$. Then $h = 400 - 16t^2 = 400 - 16\left(\frac{7}{2}\right)^2 = 400 - 16\left(\frac{49}{4}\right) = 400 - 4(49) = 400 - 196 = 204$.

42. A

Triangle *XYZ* is a right triangle. The legs of this right triangle are 18 and 24. You could use the Pythagorean theorem to find the length of *XZ*, but it is faster to find the length of *XZ* by realizing that triangle *XYZ* is a special right triangle. Notice that $18 = 6 \times 3$ and $24 = 6 \times 4$. So this right triangle is a multiple of the special 3-4-5 right triangle with each member of the 3 : 4 : 5 ratio multiplied by 6. So hypotenuse *XZ* of right triangle *XYZ* is $6 \times 5 = 30$. The perimeter of triangle *XYZ* is $18 + 24 + 30 = 72$.

43. A

Notice that if we subtract the corresponding sides of the two equations, the *b* terms will cancel and we will be left with an equation with just the variable *a*. Then

$$-\begin{array}{r} 5a + b = 12 \\ (3a + b = 4) \\ \hline \end{array}$$

Since $2a = 8$, $a = 4$.

44. B

Re-express Column A to make it easier to compare to Column B.

$\dfrac{12}{1.24} \times \dfrac{100}{100} = \dfrac{1200}{124}$. Since $\dfrac{1200}{120}$ would equal 10, $\dfrac{1200}{124}$ must equal a little less than 10.

45. A

Drop a perpendicular from point (c, d) to the *x*-axis. This perpendicular will meet the *x*-axis on the negative portion of the *x*-axis.

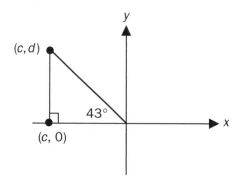

This creates a right triangle. Since two of the angles of this right triangle have degree measures of 90 and 43, the degree measure of the third interior angle of the triangle [the interior angle whose vertex is the point with the coordinates (c, d)], must be 180 − 90 − 43 = 47. In the second quadrant, where the point (c, d) is located, the *x*-coordinate of any point is negative and the *y*-coordinate of any point is positive. So *c* is negative and *d* is positive. The length of the side opposite the 43-degree angle must be *d* because *d* is positive and the length of the side opposite the 47-degree angle must be −*c* because *c* is negative. The length of the side opposite the 47-degree angle must be greater than the length of the side opposite the 43-degree angle because in a triangle a side opposite a greater angle must be greater than a side opposite a smaller angle. So −*c* > *d*, choice (A) is correct.

46. D

We are given only a non-zero restriction on the value of *y*. If $y = 1$, $-3y = -3(1) = -3$ while $5y = 5(1) = 5$. In this case Column B is greater. However, it is also possible that *y* is negative. If $y = -1$, then $-3y = -3(-1) = 3$ and $5y = 5(-1) = -5$. In this case, Column A is greater. Since different relationships between the columns are possible, choice (D) is correct.

47. D

When parallel lines are crossed by a transversal, all the acute angles are equal and all the obtuse angles are equal (unless all the angles are 90-degree angles). Also, the sum of the measures of an acute angle and an obtuse angle is 180 degrees. Here, since lines m and n are not parallel, $a + 56 \neq 180$. Therefore $a \neq 180 - 56$, that is, $a \neq 124$. If $a = 126$, then $a - 56 = 126 - 56 = 70$. In this case, Column A is greater. However, if $a = 120$, then $a - 56 = 120 - 56 = 64$. In this case, Column B is greater. Since different relationships between the columns are possible, choice (D) is correct.

48. C

If g and h are consecutive multiples of 4, the absolute difference between $g + h$ will always be 4, therefore $5(-4)^2 = 5(16) = 80$. The quantity in Column A is 80.

49. D

Be sure to consider the possibility that the centered information can be true in different ways, which would make possible different relationships between the columns.

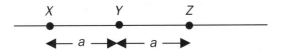

In this case the points are in the order X, Y, Z with the distance between X and Y, which we are calling a, equal to the distance between Y and Z. Here the centered information that $XZ = 2(YZ)$ is true and Column A, XY, which is a, is less than Column B, XZ, which is $2a$.

But consider another case:

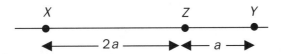

In this case, the points are in the order X, Z, and Y, We again have $XZ = 2(YZ)$ and this time Column A, XY, which is $3a$, is greater than Column B, XZ, which is $2a$.

So Column A can be less than Column B and Column A can be greater than Column B. Since different relationships between the columns are possible, choice (D) is correct.

50. B

The volume of this cube which has an edge of length e is e^3. The volume of a right circular cylinder which has a base with a radius r and a height h is $\pi r^2 h$. The base of this right circular cylinder has a diameter e. The diameter of any circle is twice the radius. So the radius of the circular base of the right circular cylinder is $\frac{e}{2}$. Let's call the height of this right circular cylinder h. Then $\pi\left(\frac{e}{2}\right)^2 h = e^3$. Now solve this equation for h in terms of e.

$$\pi\left(\frac{e}{2}\right)^2 h = e^3$$

$$\frac{\pi e^2 h}{4} = e^3$$

$$\frac{\pi h}{4} = e$$

$$\pi h = 4e$$

$$h = \frac{4e}{\pi} = \frac{4}{\pi}e$$

Column A is $\frac{4}{\pi}e$ and Column B is $\frac{4}{3}e$. Both columns contain the factor e. Since π is a little bit greater than 3 ($\pi \approx 3.14$), $\frac{4}{\pi}$ is less than $\frac{4}{3}$. Thus, Column A, $\frac{4}{\pi}e$, is less than Column B, $\frac{4}{3}e$. Choice (B) is correct.

You could have tried to solve this question by picking a number for e. Since e is the diameter of the circular base of the right circular cylinder and we will be using the radius, which is $\frac{1}{2}$ of the diameter, for finding the volume of the right circular cylinder, we should pick a value for e that is a multiple of 2. Let's let $e = 2$. Then the volume of the cube is $e^3 = 2^3 = 2 \times 2 \times 2 = 8$. So the volume of the right circular cylinder is also 8. The radius of the right circular cylinder is $\frac{e}{2} = \frac{2}{2} = 1$. If we let h be the height of the right circular cylinder, then the volume of the right circular cylinder is $\pi(1^2)h = \pi h$. So $\pi h = 8$ and $h = \frac{8}{\pi}$. The value we have for the height in Column A is $\frac{8}{\pi}$. The value that we have for Column B is $\frac{4}{3}e = \frac{4}{3}(2) = \frac{8}{3}$.

Now let's compare $\dfrac{8}{\pi}$ and $\dfrac{8}{3}$. Since π is a little bit greater than 3 ($\pi \approx 3.14$), $\dfrac{8}{\pi}$ is less than $\dfrac{8}{3}$. So in this case, Column B is greater. Choices (A) and (D) can both be eliminated. If you pick another value for e, you will again find that Column B is greater. It is not probable that there is a value for e which will give a different relationship between the columns.

51. D

Simplify Column A. $\dfrac{1}{8^k} + \dfrac{1}{8^k} + \dfrac{1}{8^k} = \dfrac{1+1+1}{8^k} = \dfrac{3}{8^k}$. Now we are comparing $\dfrac{3}{8^k}$ in Column A with $\dfrac{1}{4^k}$ in Column B. If $k = 1$, Column A is $\dfrac{3}{8^k} = \dfrac{3}{8^1} = \dfrac{3}{8}$ while Column B is $\dfrac{1}{4^k} = \dfrac{1}{4^1} = \dfrac{1}{4} = \dfrac{2}{8}$. In this case, Column A is greater. If we let $k = 2$, Column A is $\dfrac{3}{8^2} = \dfrac{3}{64}$ while Column B is $\dfrac{1}{4^2} = \dfrac{1}{16} = \dfrac{4}{64}$ In this case, Column B is greater. Since different relationships between the columns are possible, choice (D) is correct.

52. A

Since $a^2 b < 0$, $a^2 b \neq 0$. When the product of a group of factors does not equal 0, no factor equals 0. So each of a and b is nonzero. The square of any nonzero number is positive. So a^2 is positive. Since a^2 must be positive while the product of a^2 and b is negative, b must be negative. Now determine whether c is positive or negative. We have $b^3 < 0$ because a negative number raised to an odd integer exponent is negative. Since b^3 is negative and the product of b^3 and c is positive, c must be negative, because only then would the product of the negative quantity b^3 and the negative quantity c be positive. Since $b < 0$ and $c < 0$, $bc > 0$ because the product of two negative numbers is positive. Column A is greater.

You could have tried to solve this question by picking numbers. Because the key to answering this question is realizing that b must be negative, if you started by picking a positive value for b, you would have realized that b cannot be positive. Once you picked a set of values for a, b, and c that is consistent with the centered information, you would find that bc is negative, that is, bc is less than 0. In that case, Column B is greater, so you could eliminate choices (A) and (C). If you picked another set of values, you would again find that Column B is greater, so with picking numbers, choice (B) is likely to be correct. We saw in the first method that choice (B) is indeed correct.

53. B

The integer x, which is $3^7 \times 5^8 \times 7^{12}$ is written by its prime factorization, since 3, 5, and 7 are all prime numbers. The prime factorization of 35 is 5×7. Looking at $3^7 \times 5^8 \times 7^{12}$, for each factor of 35 in 35^m, there must be one factor of 5 and one factor of 7. Since in $3^7 \times 5^8 \times 7^{12}$ there are 8 factors of 5 and 12 factors of 7, there can be at most 8 pairs of the factors 5 and 7 with each pair of the factors 5 and 7 making up a factor of 35, so the greatest possible value of m is 8.

54. D

Translate the information one piece at a time.

"6 reduced by 12x" means $6 - 12x$.

"the result is equal to" means =.

"14 multiplied by the sum of 5x and 8" means $14(5x + 8)$.

Putting these together, we have

$6 - 12x = 14(5x + 8)$.

55. C

A percent is a fraction. First find the fraction that 24 is of 60 and then convert that fraction to a percent. The fraction that 24 is of 60 is $\frac{24}{60}$ which can be reduced to $\frac{2}{5}$. The percent equivalent of $\frac{2}{5}$ is 40%.

56. A

Let's begin by dividing by the fraction $\frac{5^2}{5^7}$. To divide by a fraction, invert the fraction and then multiply. $\dfrac{5^3}{\left(\frac{5^2}{5^7}\right)} = 5^3 \times \frac{5^7}{5^2} = \frac{5^3 \times 5^7}{5^2}$. Now use two laws of exponents.

One law of exponents says that when you multiply powers with the same base, add the exponents and keep the same base. Algebraically, $b^x b^y = b^{x+y}$. The other law of exponents says that when you divide powers with the same base, you subtract the exponent of the numerator from the exponent of the denominator and keep the same

base. Algebraically, $\dfrac{b^x}{b^y} = b^{x-y}$ Then $\dfrac{5^3 \times 5^7}{5^2} = \dfrac{5^{3+7}}{5^2} = \dfrac{5^{10}}{5^2} = 5^{10-2} = 5^8$.

57. E

The area of any triangle is $\dfrac{1}{2}$(base)(height). Here, if *BD* is the base, then

$$\frac{1}{2}(BD)(7) = 84$$

$$7(BD) = 168$$

$$BD = 24$$

Let's let *x* be the length of *BC*. Then the length of *CD* is *2x*. Now *BD* = *BC* + *CD*. So

$$x + 2x = 24$$

$$3x = 24$$

$$x = 8$$

The length of *BC* is 8.

58. C

We can represent the numbers of freshman, sophomores, juniors, and seniors by 10*x*, 4*x*, 8*x*, and 3*x*, respectively, where *x* is an integer. Then

$$10x + 4x + 8x + 3x = 450$$

$$25x = 450$$

$$x = 18$$

The number of freshman is greater than the number of seniors by 10*x* – 3*x* = 7*x*. Since *x* = 18, the number of freshman is greater than the number of seniors by 7(18) = 126.

59. D

In 1960, the number of families maintained by a divorced woman was about 600,000. In 1990, the number was about 4,300,000. The increase was 4,300,000 – 600,000 = 3,700,000, or 3.7 million.

60. C

In 1980, the number of families headed by widowed females was about 2,500,000, and the number of families headed by divorced females was 3,000,000. Set up the equation 2,500,000 = 3,000,000x and solve for x.

$$2,500,000 = 3,000,000x$$

$$\frac{2,500,000}{3,000,000} = x$$

$$\frac{5}{6} = x$$

Since $\frac{5}{6}$ is not an answer choice, we need to find the one that comes closest to $\frac{5}{6}$. Both choices (A) and (B) are approximately $\frac{1}{2}$, which is too low. Choice (E) is greater than 1, which is too high. We can convert the remaining choices to a common denominator and compare them.

$$\frac{5}{6} = \frac{50}{60}$$

$$\frac{17}{20} = \frac{51}{60}$$

$$\frac{29}{30} = \frac{58}{60}$$

$\frac{17}{20}$ is the closest to $\frac{5}{6}$.

61. B

Percent increase = $\dfrac{\text{New value} - \text{Old value}}{\text{Old Value}}$ × 100%. In 1980, 1,750,000 families were maintained by married women with absent husbands. In 1970, the number was 1,400,000 families.

$$\text{Percent increase} = \frac{1,750,000 - 1,400,000}{1,400,000} \times 100\%$$

$$= \frac{350,000}{1,400,000} \times 100\%$$

$$= .25 \times 100\%$$

$$= 25\%$$

25% is closest to choice (B).

62. C

Looking at the chart, we can see that from 1975 to 1980, the number of families in the US maintained by a divorced woman went from approximately 2,000,000 to 3,000,000, an increase of 1,000,000.

63. A

The highest ratio will be when the number of families maintained by widowed female is the greatest above the number of families maintained by a female with an absent husband. Looking at the chart, we can see the biggest difference is in year 1960.

64. B

Check if the right triangle in the figure is a special right triangle. This triangle is a multiple of the 5/12/13 right triangle with each member of the 5/12/13 ratio multiplied by 20 (actually each member of the 5/12/13 ratio is multiplied by 20 feet). So the length of the hypotenuse, in feet, must be 13(20) = 260. The perimeter of the triangle, which is the total length of the fence, is (100 feet) + (240 feet) + (260 feet) = 600 feet. Since the weight per foot of the fence is $\dfrac{3 \text{ pounds}}{5 \text{ feet}} = \dfrac{3}{5}$ pounds per foot, the weight of the entire fence is 600 feet $\times \dfrac{3}{5}$ = 360 pounds.

65. A

Solve the inequality $y > 2y^2$.

$$y > 2y^2$$
$$2y^2 - y < 0$$
$$y(2y - 1) < 0$$

When the product of two real numbers is negative, one of the numbers is negative and the other number is positive. There are two possibilities.

(i) $y < 0$ and $2y - 1 > 0$

(ii) $y > 0$ and $2y - 1 < 0$

Consider case (i). We already have $y < 0$. Solve $2y - 1 > 0$ for y.

$$2y - 1 > 0$$
$$2y > 1$$
$$y > \dfrac{1}{2}$$

In case (i) we must have both $y < 0$ and $y > \dfrac{1}{2}$. This is impossible, so we can rule out case (i).

In case (ii) we must have both $y > 0$ and $2y - 1 < 0$. We already have that $y > 0$. Solve $2y - 1 < 0$ for y.

$$2y - 1 < 0$$

$$2y < 1$$

$$y < \frac{1}{2}$$

In case (ii) we must have both $y > 0$ and $y < \dfrac{1}{2}$. We can say that $0 < y < \dfrac{1}{2}$.

66. C

Let's label the third unmarked angle in the triangle on the right which has angles of 90 degrees and 47 degrees.

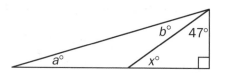

The sum of the degree measures of the interior angles of a triangle is 180 degrees. So in the triangle which has angles of $x°$, 47°, and 90°, $x + 47 + 90 = 180$, $x + 137 = 180$, and $x = 43$. The angle marked x degrees is an exterior angle of the triangle that has the two interior angles marked $a°$ and $b°$. An exterior angle of a triangle is equal to the sum of the two nonadjacent (or remote) interior angles. So $x = a + b$. Since $x = 43$, $a + b = 43$.

If you did not remember the exterior angle theorem, you could have proceeded like this. Once you found that $x = 43$, you could say that the unmarked interior angle of the triangle having the angles marked $a°$ and $b°$ has a measure of $180 - 43 = 137$ degrees. Then, since the sum of the interior angles in any triangle is 180 degrees, in the triangle with the angles marked $a°$ and $b°$, $a + b + 137 = 180$, and $a + b = 43$.

KAPLAN

67. E

First, 420 divided by 14 is 30 with no remainder, so the number of positive multiples of 14 that are less than or equal to 420 is 30. These multiples of 14 are 14(1), 14(2), 14(3), ..., 14(29), and 14(30). The prime factorization of 14 is 2×7 and the prime factorization of 35 is 5×7. So for a multiple of 14 to also be a multiple of 35, it must contain at least one prime factor of 2, one prime factor of 5, and one prime factor of 7. So a multiple of both 14 and 35 must be a multiple of $2 \times 5 \times 7 = 70$. Since 420 divided by 70 is 6 with no remainder, there are 6 multiples of 70 that are less than or equal to 420. Thus, the integers less than or equal to 420 that are multiples of both 14 and 35 are 70(1), 70(2), 70(3), 70(4), 70(5), and 70(6). These are the integers 70, 140, 210, 280, 350, and 420. So among the positive integers that are less than or equal to 420, there are 6 multiples of 14 that are also multiples of 35 and there are 30 multiples of 14. The fraction we are seeking is $\dfrac{6}{30}$ which can be reduced to $\dfrac{1}{5}$.

68. D

The smallest perfect square greater than 14 is 16, which is 4^2. The greatest perfect square less than 108 is 100, which is 10^2. Since y is to be an integer, we can write that $16 \leq y^2 \leq 100$. If y is positive, we can say that $\sqrt{16} \leq y \leq \sqrt{100}$, that is, $4 \leq y \leq 10$. However, y can also be negative. If y is a negative integer, we can say that $-\sqrt{100} \leq y \leq -\sqrt{16}$, that is, $-10 \leq y \leq -4$. All the possible values of y are -10, -9, -8, -7, -6, -5, -4, 4, 5, 6, 7, 8, 9, and 10. The greatest possible value of y is 10 and the least possible value of y is -10. Subtracting the smallest possible value from the greatest possible value, we obtain $10 - (-10) = 20$.

Section Two

GRE STUDY PLAN

CHAPTER THREE

Customize Your Study Plan

Now that you have completed the Diagnostic Exam, it is time to assess your results. By giving yourself an idea of how well you have performed, you will better be able to identify those areas in which you need help. Study time is limited, we know, so how you spend your time is crucial.

SCORE YOURSELF

There are many variables that go into how well you'll perform on the real test, and as such, there is no way to calculate a precise score. You can, however, get a ballpark idea. Go through the exam and figure out how you performed.

First, look at the **AWA**. The AWA score ranges from **0–6 (best)**. This score is an average of the two essay scores, and is totally separate from the Verbal and Quantitative scores. You can get a good idea if your essay is on the right track by reading your finished essay and comparing it to the sample essays in this book. Then, use the scoring criteria included in the Diagnostic Test Answers and Explanations (page 31) to see what elements you covered and what elements you missed. Be as objective as you can, and if you aren't sure, ask someone whose opinion you respect to read your essay as well. Though this method isn't as precise as the official essay grading system, it's close, and it will give you a better idea of how to focus your essay practice in the weeks ahead.

Second, turn to the multiple-choice answers. Tally the number of questions you got right in the Verbal and Quantitative Sections. (Hopefully you answered every question, since on the real CAT, you won't be able to skip a question.) Use the chart on the following page to get an idea of how well you did.

For these two sections, scores range from **200–800**. Two-thirds of test takers score between 400 and 600.

GRE SCORE CONVERSION CHART

Number of questions answered correctly in each section	Scaled Subscore Quantitative	Subscore Percentile Quantitative	Scaled Subscore Verbal	Subscore Percentile Verbal
0	200	0	200	0
1	200	1	200	0
2	200	1	200	0
3	200	1	200	0
4	210	1	200	0
5	240	1	200	0
6	270	1	200	0
7	310	3	220	1
8	340	6	240	1
9	370	9	260	3
10	400	14	280	5
11	420	17	300	7
12	450	23	310	9
13	470	27	330	12
14	490	32	350	16
15	520	39	360	18
16	540	43	380	24
17	560	48	400	28
18	580	53	410	31
19	610	60	430	37
20	630	(64)	450	43
21	650	68	470	49
22	670	73	480	52
23	690	77	500	57
24	710	80	520	63
25	730	84	540	68
26	750	88	560	73
27	770	92	580	78
28	780	93	610	83
29	800	96	630	86
30	800	96	650	89
31	na	na	670	92
32	na	na	700	95
33	na	na	720	96
34	na	na	740	98
35	na	na	770	99
36	na	na	790	99
37	na	na	800	99
38	na	na	800	99

The scoring for this Diagnostic Test is based on one half of a normal-length test.

IDENTIFY YOUR WEAK AREAS

Now it's time to review how well you did on each question type. By doing this, you will be able to build a customized study plan.

Analytical Writing Assessment: 2 essays

There are many ways to turn a good essay into a great essay, but the best way is through focused practice with test-like prompts. To find appropriate prompt topics, turn to the op-ed page in your local newspaper and find an issue or an argument to write about. Or you can check out *www.gre.org/stuwrit.html* for sample prompts. Before you write, keep in mind the following things:

- If possible, type your essays into a computer. Any basic word-processing program will do. As you know, the GRE is a computer-based test, so you'll want to practice under the same circumstances.

- When you sit down to write your essays, make sure you have an alarm clock on hand. For the Issue essay, set it to ring after 45 minutes. For the Argument essay, set it to ring after 30 minutes. Make sure to do both essays in the same sitting. These are the first tasks you will be required to do on test day. (Note that the exact order doesn't matter, as that will be random on test day.)

- Always spend a few minutes creating an outline for your essay. You'll be sorry if you jump in and just start typing.

- When you complete your essay(s), put it away for a few days before you assess it. A fresh eye is key for proper evaluation. How convincing is your case? Is your discussion clear and do you see progression from start to end? Compare your text to the GRE rubric provided on pages 31–32.

Try another prompt the following week to see how you have progressed. You're sure to improve if you dedicate time to practice writing a winning GRE-style essay.

Sentence Completion: 6 questions

You will see 6 Sentence Completion questions, which account for about 20 percent of your Verbal score. Sentence Completion questions test your knowledge of the rules of sentence structure and the breadth of your vocabulary. Sentence Completion questions test your ability to choose from five responses the best word(s) or phrase(s) that best complete the sentence, based on the rules of standard written English. Tally how many of these questions you got right.

If you answered 5-6 questions correctly:

You have a great understanding of the structure of sentences and a strong vocabulary. Clearly, this is an area of strength for you. Skim over the few questions you did miss and try to grasp why. Check to see that you didn't make careless errors.

If you answered 3-4 questions correctly:

You're solid in this area but could use some review. Look at the questions you answered incorrectly. Check the sentence for key words you may have missed, such as *since, similarly, thus, likewise, therefore, despite, unless, rather, while, unfortunately,* or *nonetheless.*

If you answered 0–2 questions correctly:

Reviewing the fundamentals of sentence structure and building your vocabulary need to be top priorities. Go back to the basics: verb usage; use of pronouns and modifiers; parallel structure. Strengthen your vocabulary by quizzing yourself with GRE vocabulary flashcards, studying word families and roots, and reading books or other materials with challenging words used in context (such as high-level publications like the *Wall Street Journal* and the New York *Times*).

Analogies: 8 questions

Analogies make up about 30 percent of the Verbal questions. Like all the other Verbal question types, Analogies test your vocabulary skills. But also, you have to know how to discern the relationship between two words or phrases. Tally how many of these questions you got right.

If you answered 7–8 questions correctly:

You're in great shape. Clearly, you have a great vocabulary and a solid understanding of how words relate. Skim over the question or two that you missed and try to understand what happened. Just spend a bit of time challenging yourself with new words, and you'll be well-prepared for test day.

If you answered 4–6 questions correctly:

You have some understanding of Analogies but you need to strengthen your word knowledge. There are some tough words on the GRE. Chances are, you didn't know what some of them meant. Push yourself to learn new words—challenging words. Review the concepts of word families and roots. Read materials with tough words used in context (such as high-level publications like the *Wall Street Journal* and the New York *Times*). Quiz yourself with GRE vocabulary flashcards.

You'll also need to strengthen your understanding of bridges in the Analogies questions. A bridge defines the true relationship between two words. Practice making your own analogies, and be sure to clarify the bridge.

If you answered 0–3 questions correctly:

You need to go back to the basics. That means strengthening your vocabulary (yes, memorizing new words) and learning the principles of bridge-building. Analogies are, first and foremost, about what words mean, so you'll have to learn lots of new ones. Shoot to learn two new words a day.

With respect to bridge-building, focus on understanding how two words relate. Take the words *airplane* and *hangar*, for instance, the function of a hangar is to store airplanes. That's a *function/purpose* bridge. A correct analogy is an analogy that expresses a strong bridge between two words. Practice taking two related words and building a bridge between them.

Go back to the Analogy questions on the Diagnostic. Try to reassess the bridges between each pair of words. See if you fell for the *both are* bridge trap: This type of relationship—where both words are **not** related to each other but **only** to a third word—are **never** be a correct answer choice on the GRE.

Antonyms: 9 questions

Antonyms will account for about 30 percent of your Verbal score. Antonyms test the breadth of your vocabulary and your ability to identify true opposites. Tally how many of these questions you got right.

If you answered 7–9 questions correctly:

You have a strong vocabulary. Clearly, this is an area of strength for you. Skim over the few words you did miss and try to understand why.

If you answered 4–6 questions correctly:

You're solid in this area but could use some review. Look at the questions you missed. Brush up on your vocabulary, word roots, and families. Remember to **eliminate all answer choices that do not have a clear opposite**. Words often have subtle meanings, and figuring out whether there are two direct opposites can be tricky.

If you answered 0–3 questions correctly:

Strengthening your vocabulary needs to be a top priority. Try quizzing yourself with GRE vocabulary flashcards, studying word families and roots, and reading books or other materials with GRE words used in context (such as high-level publications like the *Wall Street Journal* and the New York *Times*).

Remember to use the positive and negative charges of words to help you work through this section. And remember to eliminate all answer choices that do not have a clear opposite.

Reading Comprehension: 7 questions

There are two reading passages on the test, each followed by 3–4 questions. The passages are written in difficult, often technical prose, and are adapted from books and journals in the broad areas of business, the social sciences, and the natural sciences. These questions are designed to test whether you can read for the gist of the prose—its underlying purpose and principal ideas—quickly and accurately.

Reading Comprehension is the most time-consuming question type, and for many test-takers, the most intimidating part of the Verbal section. This doesn't have to be the case.

Despite what many test-takers seem to believe, Reading Comprehension questions do not test your ability to read and comprehend a passage so thoroughly that you practically memorize what you read. Nor do they test your ability to relate what you read to outside knowledge. And they most definitely do not test your ability to offer a creative or original analysis of what you read. What they demonstrate is test your ability to understand the substance of the passage and, where necessary, to research the passage for specific information. Tally how many of these questions you got right.

If you answered 6–7 questions correctly:

You're in great shape. You are masterful at being able to understand the substance of a passage and to research a passage for specific information. Clearly, you have a talent for understanding reading texts. Skim over the questions you missed, and try to understand why.

If you answered 3–5 questions correctly:

You need some work in the area of Reading Comprehension. Review the questions you missed, going back to the original reading passage as needed. Maybe you misread something. Maybe you skipped an important detail. Being able to distinguish opinions or interpretations from factual assertions is important in Reading Comprehension.

If you answered 0–2 questions correctly:

You'll need to learn to home in on the "why" and the "how" of a text. Those two things make GRE reading different from everyday reading. Re-read the passages on the questions you missed. Start off focusing on the author's views. What is the main idea? Examine how each paragraph fits in to the overall scope of the passage. Then, practice making a road map—handwritten notes on your scratch paper indicating the general idea. Don't sweat the details, as they won't be significant for answering the questions.

Problem Solving/Data Interpretation: 14 questions

Problem Solving/Data Interpretation questions consist of approximately 9 of the classic multiple-choice math problems found on many standardized tests and approximately 5 questions relating to a graph or chart. The math tested on these questions consists mainly of junior and senior high-school-level arithmetic, algebra, and geometry, along with median/mode/range, standard deviation, and simple probability. This section counts for about half of your Quantitative score. Tally how many of these questions you got right.

If you answered 11–14 questions correctly:

This section should give you little trouble on test day. Skim over the questions you missed and try to understand why.

If you answered 5–10 questions correctly:

You need a more focused and careful review in this area. Go back to the questions and try to figure out how you did. Look at the questions you answered correctly and review how you came up with the right answer. Ask yourself: Did you simply know the answer offhand? Did you make an educated guess? Review briefly the basic concepts of math.

If you answered 0–4 questions correctly:

Your problem solving and data interpretation skills need work. Review basic math concepts. Then go back and learn to develop a systematic approach to the questions in this section. Decide how much effort to put into each question. Learn to get comfortable using alternative methods, such as Picking Numbers or Backsolving, where you plug answer choices into the question to see which one works.

Quantitative Comparisons (QCs): 14 questions

Quantitative Comparisons account for half of your Quantitative score. The basic task here is to compare two quantities. The answer choices in this section are always the same.

The math topics tested on QCs are the same as those tested on Problem Solving/Data Interpretation questions: junior and senior high-school level arithmetic, algebra, and geometry, along with median/mode/range, standard deviation, and simple probability. Tally how many of these questions you got right.

If you answered 11–14 questions correctly:

You're in great shape. Clearly, QCs are a strength of yours. Skim over the questions you missed and try to understand what went wrong.

If you answered 5–10 questions correctly:

You need some work in this area. Review those questions that gave you the greatest difficulty. Maybe you just need a refresher in math. Review the following topics: ratios/rates/percentages; median/mode/range; algebra; number properties; geometry; standard deviation; simple probability.

If you answered 0–4 questions correctly:

QCs are difficult for you, but don't fret: you aren't alone. They're difficult for most students. Make this a high priority in your review. First, learn the answer choices (A) through (D) cold. They are always the same. You've got to become familiar with them now so that you can minimize errors on test day. Second, learn the proper plan of attack for a QC: that means making both columns look alike and then doing the same thing to each. Third, learn what traps to avoid. Don't make erroneous assumptions or forget to consider all the possibilities.

BUILD YOUR STUDY PLAN

Now that you have reviewed all the question types and assessed your skill set, it's time to implement your study plan. To do this, you'll need to map out your objectives in a calendar. We'll help you nail down your study schedule in the next chapter.

CHAPTER FOUR

Customize Your Study Schedule

Maybe you have plenty of time to devote to studying for the GRE. Maybe you're such a whiz with quantitative comparisons that you barely need to review. Maybe, though, you're like most people, and you need to make a study plan.

The key to effective test prep goes beyond practice quizzes; it starts with planning. To get you from today to test day, we're going to work with your diagnostic test results and come up with a study plan that works for you—tailored to your skills and timetable.

STEP 1: HOW MANY MONTHS UNTIL THE GRE?

On page 80 at the end of this chapter, you'll find a blank calendar. The page shows only one month, so if you have more time than that, photocopy it for every month you have. Ideally, you should have three full months to study. If you have less than two months to prepare, however, don't despair; just get going on your study plan today.

STEP 2: HOW MUCH REAL TIME DO I HAVE TO STUDY?

It's easy to think that if you have three months to study, you're all set. That's all the time in the world, right? Not likely. You probably have a job or school to factor in, as well as other time-consuming obligations. And don't forget your social life!

That said, let's give your calendar a good look. Block out the time you are at work or school. Next, block out any weekly meetings you have, remembering to include volunteer work, club activities, religious observances, sessions at the gym, and so on. Go ahead and write in your calendar. Carve it up and make it your own.

If you're like most busy graduate school candidates, you may not have as much time to devote to GRE prep as you thought. But the good news is that you now know exactly how much study time you have to work with. Maybe it's an hour in the evening, plus four hours straight on Sunday for the next three months. Maybe it's less. Either way, you can now approach your study time more realistically.

STEP 3: HOW SHOULD I TARGET MY STUDY TIME?

Go back to your diagnostic results. Sort the question types in order of difficulty; that is, the order of difficulty that *you* experienced. Focus first on the types that gave you the most trouble. Then, focus on the subsequent types as they appear on your list.

Of course the focus should be on the questions types you found challenging, but don't dismiss those you found easy. When you need a break from the troublesome questions, put them on hold and review the questions you aced. The power of review goes a long way, even if you think you know the subject matter through and through.

In the chapters that follow, you will find practice quizzes for each GRE question type. Go right to the question type that gave you the most trouble. Complete the skill-building quiz for that topic in Week 1. Analyze your results. Compare them with how you performed on the Diagnostic Test. Did you improve? We hope so. If you still need more practice, Kaplan offers a comprehensive preparation guide to the GRE, available at Borders. Check out your local store.

Also in Week 1, consider the broader topics areas you may see on the Quantitative and Verbal sections of the test. You may be shaky on antonyms or obtuse angles. Make flashcards to drill yourself on math rules, word roots, and vocabulary to help you hone your skills in these areas. (Kaplan makes these, too, available exclusively at Borders.) We provide a tear-out reference sheet in the front of the book for studying on the go. Tear it out and bring it with you whenever possible. Five-minute capsule reviews here and there can add up.

In Week 2, review what you studied in Week 1. Add some flashcard practice, then tackle another practice chapter—this time on your second weakest section.

For Week 3, you guessed it: review Weeks 1 and 2, build on the skills you developed by practicing with flashcards, and then plow through another practice chapter. At this point, you're well on your way to a systemic approach to conquering the GRE.

For each of the remaining weeks until test day, take on another chapter from this book. If you don't make it through the whole way, that's okay—you've already mastered your weakest areas. Don't wait until the last month to try the Analytical Writing section, though. It takes time to develop the skills required for this. Take a stab at the Analytical Writing prompts we include here, and then review your essay based on the grading rubric provided.

It's a good idea to take another practice test before the real exam—ideally, just one week before. Try out the official test prep from ETS, the maker of the GRE. Log onto *www.gre.org* and see what study tools are available to you.

STEP 4: WHERE'S THE BEST PLACE TO STUDY?

OK, so you know when you can study, but what about where? Some people require silence, others prefer white noise. Go where you will optimize your study time. Bear in mind, though, if it takes 20 minutes to get to your favorite study location, you're cutting into valuable study time. Pick a location that's close by.

STEP 5: AM I READY FOR THE GRE?

First of all, the fact that you have set up a study schedule and stuck to it is commendable. That's more than most students do, and the discipline you applied here will prove to be invaluable on test day. If you suffer a lapse of focus, remember your goals. Your hard work is going to pay off one day when you are accepted into graduate school.

Many of us feel unsure of our test-taking abilities. We all know the feeling of walking confidently into an exam only to blank out at the start of the test. Maybe that's never happened, but you're thinking that it could. If you find yourself thinking thoughts like that, just put a stop to it, immediately.

If you must dwell on something in the middle of the night, dwell on an image of yourself calmly answering questions correctly on test day. Imagine feeling good when you walk out of the test room. Think about the progress you're making on your study schedule, or just get out of bed and run through a few flashcards. You are preparing for this exam, and that means you will pass.

As mentioned, one or two weeks before you take the GRE, wake up early on a Saturday and take a final practice test. Notice your improvement from the diagnostic test you took at the start of this book. Then go back over your notes, flashcards, and tear-out sheet in the days ahead. Expectations tend to be fulfilled. Be positive: think about the progress you have made. You surely will have strengthened your skills after working through this book.

One last thing: Don't cram the night before the test. Get a good night's sleep. You'll wake up prepared and ready to succeed on the GRE. Good luck!

STUDY CALENDAR

Make a copy of this page for every month of study. Fill it out. Stick to it!

Month: _____

Sunday	Monday	Tuesday	Wednesday	Thursday	Friday	Saturday

CHAPTER FIVE

Countdown to the Test

It's no secret that preparation plays a huge role in test success. If you're aiming to ace any sort of exam, you'll undoubtedly invest time in learning the test layout, familiarizing yourself with question types and reviewing important content. A critical part of effective preparation, too, is knowing the environmental set-up ahead of time. You must manage natural Test Day jitters, and you have to be able to overcome challenges presented by factors that are out of your control—noise, temperature, security issues, and, in the case of the GRE, the particular hurdles presented by the computer-adaptive test format, among other things.

You will be taking the GRE at a test center. There, you'll be assigned a private computer work station. You can expect to be there for approximately four hours.

COME PREPARED

Make sure to arrive 20–30 minutes before your scheduled test time for check-in procedures. You'll need to present valid ID at the test center. Your ID must be current and contain the following:

* Your name exactly as provided when you made your test appointment
* A recent, recognizable photograph
* Your signature

If the name on your ID doesn't match the name on your test appointment, the test administrator will have the right to turn you away. So when you register to take your exam, be sure that you give the name is consistent in both places. Check *www.gre.org* for a list of acceptable forms of ID.

Additionally, you will be asked to sign a confidentiality statement at the test center. Your signature is required. If you do not sign the statement, you will not be permitted to take the test and you will forfeit your test fee.

Remember to bring your authorization voucher if you registered by mail.

WHAT NOT TO BRING

You will not be permitted to use "testing aids" during the test session or during breaks. So leave the following at home (or in your locker):

- Notes
- Scratch paper
- A calculator
- A stopwatch or watch alarm
- A cell phone
- Pens or other writing utensils (they're provided at the test center)
- A ruler
- A dictionary

WHAT NOT TO DO

Test conditions are strict. The test administrator is authorized to dismiss you for:

- Attempting to take the test for someone else
- Failing to provide acceptable identification
- Creating a disturbance
- Giving or receiving unauthorized help
- Eating or drinking during the test
- Using test aids of any kind
- Accessing your locker during the exam
- Exceeding the time permitted for scheduled breaks
- Leaving the test center
- Attempting to remove scratch paper from the testing room
- Attempting to tamper with the operation of the computer
- Attempting to remove test questions from the testing room
- Refusing to follow directions

THE SCOOP ON SCRATCH PAPER

The administrator will provide you with six sheets of scratch paper that may be replaced after you have used them all. You may not remove this paper from the testing room. All scratch paper must be returned at the end of the test session. You may not take your own scratch paper into the testing room.

KAPLAN

SOME IMPORTANT FACTS ABOUT COMPUTERIZED TESTING

CAT stands for computer-adaptive test. What this means is that the computer will determine whether to increase or decrease the level of questions depending on how well you are doing within each section. For that reason, answering early questions correctly is vital for a good score. Hard questions are worth more than easy questions.

You cannot skip a question. Even if you're having trouble figuring something out, you'll have to make your best guess and then move on to the next question. Also, you are not allowed to go back and check earlier answers, so choose your answers quickly and carefully.

You may be penalized more heavily for not getting to a question at all than for answering it incorrectly. So even if you only have a minute or two left in a section, you should guess at random rather than leave questions unanswered.

Good luck!

Section Three

GRE SKILL-BUILDING QUIZZES

CHAPTER SIX

Problem Solving/
Data Interpretation

PROBLEM SOLVING/DATA INTERPRETATION QUIZ

Directions: Select the best of the five answer choices given.

Questions 1-5 refer to the following table and graph.

AVERAGE DAILY SALES AND LOT SIZE AT DEALERSHIP *Y*
FOR CARS MADE BY FIVE COMPANIES

Car Manufacturer	Average Daily Sales (thousands)	Percent of Total Average Daily Sales	Lot Area (Square Feet)	Average Daily Sales per Square Foot of Lot Area
A	$3		15,000	$0.2000
B		16%	7,500	$0.2666
C	$1.5	12%		
D	$2	16%	10,000	
E			7,500	$0.5333
Total	$12.5	100%		

The following diagram represents 5 identical lots at Dealership *Y* and the size of each car manufacturer's space per lot.

DISTRIBUTION OF LOT SIZE FOR FIVE CAR-MANUFACTURERS
AT DEALERSHIP *Y*

	A	*B*	*C*	*D*	*E*
Lot 1	3,000 ft.²	1,500 ft.²	1,000 ft.²	2,000 ft.²	1,500 ft.²
Lot 2					
Lot 3					
Lot 4					
Lot 5					

1. In dealership *Y*, what is the total area, in square feet, of the lots that sell cars manufactured by company *C*?

   (A) 1,000

   (B) 5,000

   (C) 6,000

   (D) 7,500

   (E) 12,000

2. What is the average daily sales per square foot of lot area for cars manufactured by company *D*?

   (A) $0.08

   (B) $0.10

   (C) $0.16

   (D) $0.20

   (E) $0.32

3. Car manufacturer *E*'s average daily sales are what percent of the total average daily sales of cars from the five car manufacturers at dealership *Y*?

   (A) 8%

   (B) 16%

   (C) 24%

   (D) 32%

   (E) It cannot be determined from the information given.

4. If the lot sizes for cars from manufacturers *A* and *B* were reversed and their average daily sales <u>per square foot</u> remained the same, then the total average daily sales would do which of the following?

   (A) Decrease by $1,500.

   (B) Decrease by $1,000.

   (C) Remain unchanged.

   (D) Increase by $500.

   (E) Increase by $1,000.

5. In dealership *Y*, lot 1 accounted for $\frac{1}{3}$ of car manufacturer *C*'s average daily sales, and lot 2 accounted for $\frac{3}{5}$ as much as lot 1. If lots 4 and 5 each accounted for less than lot 2, but together accounted for more than lot 1, then which of the following could have been the average daily sales from lot 3 of cars manufactured by company *C*?

   (A) $70

   (B) $90

   (C) $125

   (D) $210

   (E) $245

6. $(10 - 9 - 8) - (9 - 8 - 7 - (8 - 7 - 6)) =$

   (A) −8

   (B) −6

   (C) −2

   (D) 2

   (E) 4

7. If $8z - 12 = 44$, then $5z =$

   (A) 7

   (B) 10

   (C) 20

   (D) 30

   (E) 35

8. Shelly has 17 toys, consisting of 6 balls, 4 trucks, 5 stuffed animals and 2 dolls. Each day on her way to school, her father lets her take one of each kind of toy with her in the car. How many trips to school can Shelly take without repeating a particular group of toys?

   (A) 17

   (B) 120

   (C) 180

   (D) 240

   (E) 720

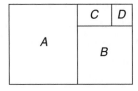

Note: Figure not drawn to scale.

9. In the figure above, there are two squares, A and B, and two rectangles, C and D. If the perimeter of A is 32, the area of B is 36, and the area of D is 2, then what is the area of C?

   (A) 8

   (B) 10

   (C) 12

   (D) 14

   (E) 16

10. In a certain economics class, 65 of the students scored 70 or below on a test. If 40 students scored at least 55, then which of the following could NOT be the class median score?

    (A) 50

    (B) 60

    (C) 62

    (D) 69

    (E) 75

11. The product of two positive numbers is $12yz + 4y^2$. The larger number is $4y$. What is the difference between the larger number and the smaller number?

    (A) $5y - 3z$

    (B) $3(y - z)$

    (C) $4y - 3z - 1$

    (D) $3z + y$

    (E) $3(z - y)$

12. A square box with a side length of 5 feet contains two drums. Each drum is a right circular cylinder with a radius of 1 foot and a height of 3 feet. In cubic feet, what is the volume of the box that is NOT occupied by the drums?

    (A) $25 - 6\pi$

    (B) $125 - 6\pi$

    (C) $125 - 3\pi$

    (D) $150 - 6\pi$

    (E) $150 - 3\pi$

13. In the figure above, the rectangle is inscribed in the circle. What is the area of the circle?

    (A) 5π

    (B) 10π

    (C) 25π

    (D) 28π

    (E) 48π

$$3x - y + 2z = 0$$

$$2x + 2y + 6z = 0$$

14. In the system of equations above, if $z \neq 0$, then the ratio of x to z is

    (A) $-\dfrac{5}{4}$

    (B) $-\dfrac{1}{4}$

    (C) $\dfrac{1}{4}$

    (D) $\dfrac{3}{5}$

    (E) $\dfrac{5}{4}$

15. The average of seven numbers is 30. When one of the seven numbers is removed, the average of the remaining numbers is 40. What is the value of the number that was removed?

    (A) −30

    (B) −25

    (C) 10

    (D) 35

    (E) 40

16. A high school raised money for school activities. One-half of the money went to the senior class, and then the other 3 classes divided the remaining money equally. If the junior and senior classes had $2,400 after they combined their money, how much (total) money did the high school raise?

    (A) $1,800

    (B) $3,600

    (C) $4,800

    (D) $5,400

    (E) $7,200

17. $\frac{11}{3} \times 10^{-2}$ is closest to:

    (A) 0.003667

    (B) 0.03667

    (C) 0.3667

    (D) 36.67

    (E) 366.7

18. An integer is a multiple of 7 and a multiple of 8. Which of the following must be true?

    I. The integer is a multiple of 28

    II. The integer cannot be even

    III. The integer is equal to 56

    (A) I only

    (B) II only

    (C) III only

    (D) I and II only

    (E) I, II and III

19. If k is not equal to 0, then $\dfrac{k^4}{(k^4)^3(3k)} =$

    (A) $\dfrac{1}{3k^9}$

    (B) $\dfrac{1}{k^9}$

    (C) $\dfrac{1}{3k^8}$

    (D) $\dfrac{1}{k^8}$

    (E) $\dfrac{1}{3k}$

ANSWER KEY

1. B	11. B
2. D	12. B
3. D	13. E
4. D	14. A
5. C	15. A
6. B	16. B
7. E	17. B
8. D	18. A
9. B	19. A
10. E	

PROBLEM SOLVING/DATA INTERPRETATION
ANSWERS AND EXPLANATIONS

1. B

In the second figure, we can see that cars manufactured by company *C* occupy five lots, each with 1,000 square feet of space. So the cars made by company *C* occupy a total of

$5 \times 1,000 = 5,000$ square feet of space.

2. D

We are being asked to calculate an average – apply the definition and get the data needed from the table:

average daily sales per square foot

$$= \frac{\text{amount of daily sales of } D \text{ cars}}{\text{number of square feet of } D \text{ lots}}$$

$$= \frac{\$2000}{10,000 \text{ square feet}}$$

$= \$0.20$ per square foot.

3. D

The question is asking for the entry in the "Percent of Total Average Daily Sales" column in the table for cars made by manufacturer *E*. Since sales of company *E*'s cars average $0.5333 per day per square foot, and the five lots use 7,500 square feet total, the total average daily sales of cars made by company *E* is: $0.5333 × 7,500 = $4,000. Since the total average daily sales for all cars in the dealership is $12,500, the percentage of that total accounted for by sales of cars made by manufacturer E is:

$$\frac{\$4,000}{\$12,500} \times 100\% = 4 \times \frac{100}{12.5}\% = 4 \times 8\% = 32\%$$

4. D

Before, the average daily sales of company *A*'s cars was $3,000, and the average daily sales of company *B*'s cars was $0.2666 × 7,500 = $2,000; together, that equals $5,000 of average daily sales.

If the lot sizes are reversed for *A* and *B*, then the new average daily sales of *A* cars is $0.2 × 7,500 = $1,500, and the new average daily sales of *B* cars is $0.2666 × 15,000 = $4,000; combined, the new average daily sales of both types of car is $5,500. This represents an increase of $500 over the old figures.

5. C

Cars made by manufacturer *C* average $1,500 in sales every day. According to the question, lot 1 accounts for $\frac{1}{3}$ × $1,500 = $500 of those sales. Lot 2 accounts for $\frac{3}{5}$ × $500 = $300 in sales. So far, $800 of the $1,500 has been accounted for, leaving $700 for the remaining 3 lots. Lot 4 and lot 5 accounted for less than lot 2, that is, less than $300 each. So, the maximum that lots 4 and 5 contributed together is $600, which means that lot 3 must have contributed at least $100. Also lots 4 and 5 together accounted for more than lot 1, $500, which means that the sales in lot 3 were at most $200.

Now we know that, given the conditions of the problem, sales in lot 3 must have been between $100 and $200. The only answer choice that falls in this range is choice (C), $125.

6. B

This question requires us to follow the order of operations (PEMDAS) and simplify correctly. Begin with first set of parentheses: (10 − 9 − 8) = (−7).

Then simplify the next set of parentheses. When we have parentheses inside parentheses, begin with the innermost set. Here, (8 − 7 − 6) becomes (− 5). So the second set of parentheses can be simplified to (9 − 8 − 7 − (− 5)). This becomes (9 − 8 − 7 + 5) which equals (−1).

Now we are left with (−7) − (−1) = −7 + 1 = −6. (B) is correct.

7. E

The direct approach to this problem is to solve for z and then multiply by 5. We have $8z - 12 = 44$, so we can add 12 to both sides to get $8z = 56$. Now divide both sides by 8 to get $z = 7$.

Be careful here. Notice that we are asked to solve for $5z$, not for z. If $z = 7$, then $5z = 5 \times 7 = 35$. (E) is correct. Note that choice (A) gives the value of z itself, which is a trap answer.

8. D

This is a permutation problem, because the order in which Shelly chooses her toys does not matter. For example, choosing a certain ball and then a truck is no different from selecting the truck first and then the ball. Each group of toys, consisting of 1 ball, 1 truck, 1 animal and 1 doll, will be 1 permutation.

So, to calculate the number of permutations, we just multiply the number of possibilities for each toy: 6 balls $\times$ 4 trucks $\times$ 5 animals $\times$ 2 dolls = $6 \times 4 \times 5 \times 2 = 240$ permutations. Since Shelly has 240 different possible groups, she can make 240 trips without repeating a group. (D) is correct.

9. B

C is a rectangle, so we need both its height and width in order to find its area. Based on the figure, we can see that the height of C is the difference between the height of A and the height of B. Similarly, the width of C is the difference between the width of B and the width of D. So, let's try to find the dimensions of A, B and D.

Since the perimeter of square A is 32, its dimensions must be 8 by 8 because the perimeter of a square is equal to 4 times the length of one of its sides and $32 = 4 \times 8$. Since the area of square B is 36, its dimensions are 6 by 6. So, the height of C is $8 - 6 = 2$.

From the figure, C and D have the same height, so the height of D is also 2. Since D is a rectangle with area of 2, its width must be 1 so that area = width $\times$ height = $1 \times 2 = 2$.

The width of B is 6 and the width of D is 1, so the width of C is $6 - 1 = 5$. We already know that the height of C is 2. Therefore, C is a 2 by 5 rectangle, which means it has an area of 10. (B) is correct.

Choice (D) is the perimeter of *C*. Be sure to know the difference between area and perimeter on Test Day!

10. E

The median is the middle score, the score such that half the class scored higher and half scored lower. We don't know how many students are in the class, so we can't calculate the actual median. Instead, let's work with the choices to see if we can find one that could NOT be the median. This is a "which of the following" question, so let's start with choice (E).

If the median is 75, then half the class scored above 75 and half scored below. Since 65 students scored 70 or below, we know that at least 65 students scored below 75. So, 75 could be the median only if at least 65 students scored **above** 75. But only 40 students scored above 55, so it's not possible that 65 students scored above 75. Therefore 75 cannot be the median and (E) is correct.

11. B

We're told that $4y$ times an unknown number is $12yz + 4y^2$. We can write this as $4y(\quad) = 12yz + 4y^2$ where the blank space represents the unknown number. How do we know what goes in the blank space? If we factor $4y$ out of $12yz + 4y^2$, we'll have $4y$ times *something* on both sides of the equation.

$4y(3z + y) = 12yz + 4y^2$. So, $12yz + 4y^2$ is the product of $4y$ and $(3z + y)$.

We need the difference between two numbers, and we know that $4y$ is the larger number. Thus, the difference we need is $4y - (3z + y) = 4y - 3z - y = 3y - 3z = 3(y - z)$. This is choice (B).

Another approach is to let some other variable such as x represent the unknown number. This gives us $4y(x) = 12yz + 4y^2$. Now just divide both sides by $4y$ to find that $x = 3z + y$. The difference we need is $4y - x$, or $4y - (3z + y)$, which is $3y - 3z$, or $3(y - z)$.

12. B

We need the area that is NOT occupied by the drums, which is the volume of the box minus the volume of the drums.

The volume of a square box (a cube) is the product of the three sides, or $5 \times 5 \times 5 = 125$ cubic feet.

The formula for the volume of a right circular cylinder is $\pi r^2 h$, where r is the radius and h the height. So, for one of the drums, the volume is $\pi(1)^2(3) = 3\pi$. There are 2 drums, so the total volume is $2(3\pi) = 6\pi$ cubic feet.

Thus, the unoccupied volume of the box is $125 - 6\pi$. Choice (B) is correct

13. C

Because the rectangle is inscribed in the circle, the diagonal of the rectangle must be the diameter of the circle, which is twice the radius. If we can solve for the length of the diagonal, we can then calculate the area of the circle.

Draw the figure to show the diagonal:

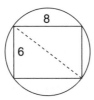

We can see that the diagonal is also the hypotenuse of a right triangle where the sides are 6 and 8. Notice that $6 = 2(3)$ and $8 = 2(4)$. Thus, the triangle is a multiple of the 3-4-5 right triangle where each member of the 3:4:5 ratio is multiplied by 2. The hypotenuse must be $2(5) = 10$, and this is also the diagonal of the rectangle.

The diagonal is equal to the diameter, and the radius is half the diameter, so the radius is 5. The area of a circle is πr^2, where r is the radius, so the area of this circle is $\pi(5^2) = 25\pi$. Therefore (E) is correct.

14. A

We have three unknowns and only 2 equations, so we won't be able to solve for x and z directly. But we can solve for the ratio of x to z, which is just $\dfrac{x}{z}$.

To do so, we'll need to eliminate the y terms. Notice that if we divide both sides of the second equation by 2, we'll have $-y$ in the first equation and y in the second equation. If we then add the equations together, the y terms will drop out and we'll be left with just x and z terms. Here's how it will work:

Divide both sides of the second equation by 2 to get $x + y + 3z = 0$. Now add the 2 equations:

$$3x - y + 2z = 0$$
$$\underline{x + y + 3z = 0}$$
$$4x + 0 + 5z = 0$$

Subtract $5z$ from both sides to get $4x = -5z$. Divide both sides by 4 to get $x = \dfrac{-5z}{4}$. Finally, divide by z to get $\dfrac{x}{z} = \dfrac{-5}{4} = -\dfrac{5}{4}$. Choice (A) is correct.

15. A

The key to this problem is knowing the average formula: Average $= \dfrac{\text{Sum of the Terms}}{\text{Number of Terms}}$. Before anything is removed, we have 7 terms (7 numbers) and an average of 30. Therefore $30 = \dfrac{\text{Sum of the Terms}}{7}$, or $30(7) =$ the sum of the terms.

Since $30(7) = 210$, we know that, before removal, the 7 numbers added up to 210.

Now we take one number away and the average becomes 40. Since the average goes UP when one number is taken away, we know that the number removed must have been below the original average. Since Choices (D) and (E) are greater than the original average of 30, they can be eliminated.

With one number gone, we have $40 = \dfrac{\text{Sum of the Terms}}{6}$, or $40(6) = 240 =$ the sum of the terms. Before removal, the sum was 210; after removal the sum is 240. The sum has INCREASED, so the number removed must have been **negative**. In fact, the number removed must have been $210 - 240 = -30$. Thus, (A) is correct.

16. B

Since the three non-senior classes divided their half of the money equally, each of them got one-third of one-half of the money, or $\left(\frac{1}{3}\right)\left(\frac{1}{2}\right) = \frac{1}{6}$ of the money. So, the senior and junior classes combined total of \$2,400 is equal to one-half plus one-sixth, or $\frac{1}{2} + \frac{1}{6}$, of the total money raised. Because $\frac{1}{2} = \frac{3}{6}$, we have $\frac{1}{2} + \frac{1}{6} = \frac{3}{6} + \frac{1}{6} = \frac{4}{6} = \frac{2}{3}$. So, the junior and senior classes together got two-thirds of the total.

Thus, if x is the unknown amount of money raised, then $\left(\frac{1}{2} + \frac{1}{6}\right)x = \$2,400$, or $\left(\frac{2}{3}\right)x = 2,400$, or $x = \left(\frac{3}{2}\right)(\$2,400) = \$3,600$, which is choice (B).

Notice that we could have eliminated (A) right away because it is less than the junior and senior classes' combined funds – meaning that it must also be less than the total raised.

We also could have eliminated choices (C), (D) and (E) because they are too large. We know the senior class got half of the total AND that the senior class itself received less than \$2,400. Because the total must be twice what the seniors got, the total money raised must have been less than 2 × \$2,400 = \$4,800. Thus, any choice equal to or greater than \$4,800 cannot be correct.

17. B

The key to this problem is remembering than numbers with negative exponents actually represent fractions. In this case, $10^{-2} = \frac{1}{10^2} = \frac{1}{100}$. So, we can rewrite the original problem as $\frac{11}{3} \times \frac{1}{100}$. Now, $\frac{11}{3} = 3\frac{2}{3}$ or approximately 3.667, so the problem becomes $\frac{3.667}{100}$. Dividing by 100 means moving the decimal point 2 places to the left, so we have $\frac{3.667}{100} = 0.36677$. Choice (B) is correct.

18. A

To evaluate the statements, we'll need to know what possible values this integer could have, so let's think about what it means for an integer to be a multiple of both 7 and 8. It means that the integer's prime factors must include all the prime factors of both 7 and 8, namely 7 and (2)(2)(2). The smallest such number is (7)(2)(2)(2) = 56, so the integer must either be 56 or a multiple of 56.

Now let's look at the statements, starting with II, since it appears in the most choices. We already know that the integer must be 56 or a multiple of 56, so it must be even. Therefore the statement "the integer cannot be even" is not true. Since we know that statement II is not true, we can cross off all choices including II. This eliminates (B), (D) and (E).

Thus, either Statement I must be true, leading to choice (A), or Statement III must be true, leading to choice (C). Statement III looks simpler, so let's work with it. We saw earlier that the integer could be 56, but it could also be any multiple of 56. Thus, it does not have to be equal to 56. Statement III is not true, so we eliminate (C), meaning that choice (A), the only remaining choice, is correct. In fact, (A) must be true. Since 56 = 28 × 2 and the integer must be a multiple of 56, it must also be a multiple of 28.

19. A

Expressions such as this can be simplified by canceling like terms from the numerator and denominator and by applying the appropriate rules of exponents.

In this case, we have k^4 in both the numerator and denominator. In the denominator, k^4 actually appears three times, since it is raised to the third power. In other words, the original fraction is equal to $\dfrac{k^4}{(k^4)(k^4)(k^4)(3k)}$. Now we can easily see that one k^4 term will cancel out, leaving us with $\dfrac{1}{(k^4)(k^4)(3k)}$.

Using the rules of exponents, $(k^4)(k^4) = k^{4+4} = k^8$, so now the fraction becomes $\dfrac{1}{(k^4)(3k)}$. Since $(k^8)(3k) = 3(k^{8+1}) = 3k^9$, the fraction is $\dfrac{1}{3k^9}$, which is choice (A).

CHAPTER SEVEN
Quantitative Comparisons

QUANTITATIVE COMPARISONS QUIZ

<u>**Directions:**</u> Compare the quantities in Column A and Column B, and choose

- (A) if the quantity in Column A is greater than the quantity in Column B
- (B) if the quantity in Column B is greater than the quantity in Column A
- (C) if the two quantities are equal
- (D) if the relationship cannot be determined using the given information

Note: There are only four choices: do not choose (E). Consider the information centered above the quantities when deciding upon your choice. A variable or symbol that appears in a question means the same thing in Column A as in Column B and/or the centered information.

1.

Column A	**Column B**

A rectangular box has a volume of 100 cubic inches, a length of x inches, a width of 4 inches, and a height of 5 inches.

x	6

2.

Column A	**Column B**

Allen's age in years is twice Bill's age in years.

Bill's age in years is 5 years more than 3 times David's age in years.

Allen's age in years	Eight years more than 6 times David's age in years

3.

Column A	**Column B**

x and y are positive integers.

$$x < 7$$
$$y > 3$$

3x	4y

4.

Column A	**Column B**

$$x^2 = 25$$
$$y^3 = 125$$

x	y

5.

Column A	**Column B**
$(x + 2)(x - 2)$	$x^2 - 2$

6.

Column A	**Column B**

A student has test scores of 80, x, and y, respectively, and an average (arithmetic mean) score of 70 on the three tests.

The average (arithmetic mean) of x and y	65

7.

Column A	**Column B**
35(246)	36(245)

8.   <u>Column A</u>   <u>Column B</u>

For all real numbers x, let $x^\Delta = -x - 1$.

$((-2)^\Delta)^\Delta$ -5

9.   <u>Column A</u>   <u>Column B</u>

$$0 < a < 1$$

a^2 a

10.   <u>Column A</u>   <u>Column B</u>

The sum of all the integers from 21 to 41, inclusive.   The sum of all the integers from 23 to 42, inclusive.

11.   <u>Column A</u>   <u>Column B</u>

The greatest prime factor of 44   The greatest prime factor of 45

12.   <u>Column A</u>   <u>Column B</u>

$2y^2$ $(2y)^2$

13.   <u>Column A</u>   <u>Column B</u>

The net income of a certain business is defined by the function $x^2 - 12x + 35$, for all positive values of x, where x equals the number of items sold.

The number of items that must be sold for the net income to be zero   6

14.   <u>Column A</u>   <u>Column B</u>

a, b, and c are positive integers and $ab = c$.

b c

15.   <u>Column A</u>   <u>Column B</u>

3.4% of 998 $(2^2)(3^2)$

16.   <u>Column A</u>   <u>Column B</u>

Working at constant rates, press A can print x magazines in 0.3 hours, while press B can print 2x magazines in 1.2 hours, where x is a positive integer.

The number of magazines printed by press A in 3 hours.   The number of magazines printed by press B in 6 hours.

17. **Column A**   **Column B**

25 percent of z is 27.

z 108

18. **Column A**   **Column B**

James and Steven are the only two people in a company who sell widgets. In the previous week, the number of widgets that James sold was $\frac{2}{5}$ less than the number of widgets that Steven sold.

The fraction of the total number of widgets sold in the previous week that were sold by Steven $\frac{5}{8}$

19. **Column A**   **Column B**

Each inch on a map represents a distance of 4 miles.

The number of inches on the map that represents a distance of 28 miles   8

20. **Column A**   **Column B**

For any number of hours that a carpenter works, the carpenter is paid the same number of dollars per hour. The carpenter earned $4j$ dollars for m hours of work and the carpenter earned n dollars for $5w$ hours worked.

$20jw$ mn

21. **Column A**   **Column B**

The three integers x, y, and z have an average (arithmetic mean) of 12.

$3(x + y + z)$ 72

22. **Column A**   **Column B**

30 percent of 18   40 percent of 14

23. **Column A**   **Column B**

$a = \frac{5b}{2}$, $b = \frac{4c}{3}$ and $c = 15$

a   50

24. **Column A**   **Column B**

32% of $450   64% of $225

25.

<u>Column A</u>	<u>Column B</u>
The total savings on 15 blank cassette tapes purchased for $1.35 per tape instead of $1.49 per tape.	$1.96

26.

<u>Column A</u>	<u>Column B</u>

Cities A and B are both suburbs of Anytown. A is 5 miles due south of Anytown, and B is 12 miles due east of Anytown.

The distance between A and B	13 miles

27.

<u>Column A</u>	<u>Column B</u>

Rectangle R has a perimeter of 20.

The greatest possible area of R	The area of R if R is a square.

28.

<u>Column A</u>	<u>Column B</u>
$\dfrac{100x^2 - 1}{100}$	x^2

KAPLAN

ANSWER KEY ON FOLLOWING PAGE

ANSWER KEY

1. B

2. A

3. D

4. D

5. B

6. C

7. B

8. A

9. B

10. A

11. A

12. D

13. D

14. D

15. B

16. C

17. C

18. C

19. B

20. C

21. A

22. B

23. C

24. C

25. A

26. C

27. C

28. B

QUANTITATIVE COMPARISONS
ANSWERS AND EXPLANATIONS

1. B

The volume V of a rectangular box is related to its length l, its width w, and its height h by the formula $V = lwh$. In this problem, $V = 100$, $l = x$, $w = 4$ and $h = 5$.

Therefore, $100 = (x)(4)(5)$, $100 = 20x$, and
$x = \dfrac{100}{20} = 5$.

Column B is greater.

2. A

To make it easier to compare the columns, let's translate the given information into equations. Let Allen's age in years be A, let Bill's age in years be B, and let David's age in years be D. Then according to the centered information, $A = 2B$ and $B = 3D + 5$.

The quantity in Column A is A and the quantity in Column B is $6D + 8$. Since we want to compare A with $6D + 8$, we want to find an expression for A in terms of D. From the centered information, we know that $A = 2B$ and $B = 3D + 5$.

If we replace B in $A = 2B$ with $B = 3D + 5$, we will an equation with the variables A and D. Making this replacement, we get $A = 2(B = 3D + 5)$. Multiplying out the right side of this equation, we have $A = 6D + 10$.

So Allen's age is 10 years more than 6 times David's age in years. This is greater than 8 years more than 6 times David's age in years. Column A is greater.

3. D

Let's pick numbers for x and y. With numbers instead of variables, the columns will look more alike and be easier to compare.

If $x = 1$ and $y = 5$, then in Column A, $3 = 3(1) = 3$, while in Column B, $4y = 4(5) = 20$. In this case, Column A is greater.

Let's see if we can find a different relationship by making x as large as possible, thus making the quantity $3x$ in Column A as large as possible, and making y as small as possible, thus making the quantity $4y$ in Column B as small as possible. The greatest possible value of x is 6 and the smallest possible value of y is 4. So we will let $x = 6$ and $y = 4$. Then in Column A, $3x = 3(6) = 18$, while in Column B, $4y = 4(4) = 16$. In this case, Column B is greater.

Since different relationships between the columns are possible, the relationship between the columns cannot be determined and choice (D) is correct.

4. D

This question is testing knowledge of exponents, specifically the fact that every positive number has two square roots, with one square root being positive and one square root being negative. If $x^2 = 25$, then x is either $+5$ or -5. If $y^3 = 125$, then y can only equal $+5$. If $x = -5$ and $y = 5$, then Column B is greater. If $x = 5$ and $y = 5$, then the quantities in both columns are equal. Since different relationships between the columns are possible, the relationship between the columns cannot be determined and choice (D) is correct.

In general, when a variable is raised to a positive even power, the variable will have 2 possible values, and when a variable is raised to positive odd power, it will have only 1 possible value.

5. B

We can change Column A to look more like Column B. In general, $(a + b)(a - b) = a^2 - b^2$. Here, let $a = x$ and $b = 2$, so $(x + 2)(x - 2) = x^2 - 2^2 = x^2 - 4$. Column A is $x^2 - 4$ and Column B is $x^2 - 2$.

Since x^2 appears in both columns, we can ignore it. Thus, we just have to compare the -4 in Column A and the -2 in Column B is. Since $-4 < -2$, Column B is greater.

6. C

We don't actually need to find values for x and y; we only need their average, which is $\frac{x + y}{2}$. If we can find $x + y$, we will be able to find the average.

How can we find $x + y$? The average of the student's 3 test scores was 70, so the sum of the three scores must have been $(3)(70) = 210$, because Average $= \dfrac{\text{Sum of the Terms}}{\text{Number of Terms}}$ and (Average)(Number of Terms) = Sum of Terms.

So, the sum of the three test scores is 210. One of the 3 scores was 80, so the remaining 2 scores must be $210 - 80 = 130$. Since x and y represent the remaining 2 scores, $130 = x + y$.

Therefore, the average of x and $y = \dfrac{x + y}{2} = \dfrac{130}{2} = 65$. Column B is also 65, so the columns are equal and (C) is correct.

7. B

When we see expressions such as 35(246) that would be time-consuming to calculate, remember that we want to **compare** the columns, not **calculate** them.

First, try to make the columns look more alike. In Column A we have 35(246), which can be expressed as the equivalent 35(245 + 1), or 35(245) + 35(1).

In Column B, 36(245) can be expressed as (35 + 1)(245) or 35(245) + 1(245).

Now these expressions can be simplified to 35(245) + 35 in Column A, and 35(245) + 245 in Column B. Removing 35(245) from each side, Column A becomes 35 and Column B becomes 245. Without doing any calculations, we can see that Column B is larger.

Note that choice (D) would not be possible here, as both columns contain only numbers.

8. A

The centered information tells us what operation to perform when we see the symbol $^\Delta$. In Column A, we see this symbol twice. To evaluate this, we just remember PEMDAS and begin with the inner set of parentheses.

Since $x^\Delta = -x - 1$, $(-2)^\Delta = -(-2) - 1 = 2 - 1 = 1$.

Therefore, $((-2)^\Delta)^\Delta = (1)^\Delta = -1 - 1 = -2$.

Thus, the quantity in Column A is -2, which is greater than -5 in Column B.

9. B

Both columns contain variables, so we should pick numbers for *a* that are consistent with the centered information, $0 < a < 1$.

If $a = \frac{1}{2}$, then $a^2 = \frac{1}{4}$, which is smaller than *a*. If $a = \frac{1}{3}$, then we see that $a^2 = \frac{1}{9}$, which is also smaller. No matter what numbers are picked, Column B is always larger than Column A. If fact, the square of any positive fraction less than 1 is smaller than that fraction.

10. A

We can compare the columns piece by piece. Each column includes the sum of all the integers from 23 to 41, inclusive, so we can ignore that sum and compare what remains. For Column A, what remains is $21 + 22 = 43$, and for Column B, what remains is 42. Since 43 is greater than 42, the correct choice is (A).

11. A

Writing the prime factorization of the number in each column is a good place to start. The prime factorization of 44 is (2)(2)(11) and the prime factorization of 45 is (3)(3)(5). 11 is the greatest prime factor of 44 and 5 is the greatest prime factor of 45.

12. D

In Column B, $(2y)^2 = (2y)(2y) = 4y^2$. So, we are comparing $2y^2$ and $4y^2$. We can divide both columns by 2, so we just have y^2 and $2y^2$.

It appears that Column B is larger, but let's pick numbers to be sure. For most numbers, such as $y = 2$, or $y = -\frac{1}{2}$, Column B is larger.

If $y = 2$, then Column A = 4 and Column B = 8

If $y = -\frac{1}{2}$, then Column A = $\frac{1}{4}$ and Column B = $\frac{1}{2}$

In fact, for any non-zero value of *y*, Column B will be larger, but we can't forget about zero. If $y = 0$, the columns are equal. Therefore, the relationship between the columns cannot be determined.

13. D

To evaluate Column A, we can set the expression for net income equal to zero and solve for x. Net income is $x^2 - 12x + 35$, so we have the equation $x^2 - 12x + 35 = 0$.

Using reverse FOIL, we can factor the left side of the equation as $(x - 5)(x - 7)$. So, the equation becomes $(x - 5)(x - 7) = 0$. Either $(x - 5)$ must be zero, or $(x - 7)$ must be zero, so x could be either 5 or 7.

Therefore, the company has a net income of 0 when it sells either 5 or 7 items. If it sells 5 items, Column B is larger, but if it sells 7 items, Column A is larger. The relationship between the columns cannot be determined.

14. D

We can pick numbers here to make the situation more concrete.

Let's choose $a = 2$ and $b = 3$. Thus, $c = 6$, which would make Column B greater. However, if $a = 1$ and $b = 2$, then $c = 2$ and the columns are equal. Since we have two sets of numbers that give us different relationships, the relationship cannot be determined.

It's also possible to state both columns in terms of one variable before we compare them. Since $ab = c$, $a = \dfrac{c}{b}$, so Column A becomes $\dfrac{c}{b}$. Now c appears in both columns, so if we divide both columns by c, we are left with:

Column A: $\dfrac{1}{b}$

Column B: 1

Since p is a positive integer, $\dfrac{1}{b}$ will be equal to 1 if $p = 1$, but $\dfrac{1}{b}$ will be a fraction less than 1 if $b > 1$. Thus the relationship between the columns cannot be determined.

15. B

We should make the columns look more alike. It would take too much time to calculate 3.4% of 998, so instead let's try to express Column B as a percentage.

In Column B, $(2^2)(3^2) = (4)(9) = 36$. This is 3.6% of 1000, which is a larger percentage (3.6% vs. 3.4%) of a larger number (1000 vs. 998) than that of Column A, so Column B must be larger.

16. C

The time given for press A, three hours, is ten times longer than the 0.3 hours the press needs to print x magazines. Thus, in 3 hours, the press can print $10x$ magazines.

Press B prints $2x$ magazines in 1.2 hours. Dividing by 2, this is equivalent to x magazines in 0.6 hours. Therefore, in 6 hours, press B can print $10x$ magazines. Thus, the quantities in the two columns are equal.

We could also pick a number for x, such as $x = 6$. So press A prints $\frac{6 \text{ magazines}}{.3 \text{ hours}} = \frac{60 \text{ magazines}}{3 \text{ hours}} = \frac{20 \text{ magazines}}{\text{hour}}$. So in 3 hours, press A produces 60 magazines. Press B produces 12 magazines per 1.2 hours or 10 magazines per hour.

So in 6 hours, press B also produces 10 magazines.

17. C

The fractional equivalent of 25 percent is $\frac{1}{4}$. Thus, 25% of z is the same as $\frac{1}{4}z$. So, $\frac{1}{4}z = 27$. Multiplying both sides of this equation by 4, we have $4\left(\frac{1}{4}z\right) = 4(27)$, and $z = 108$. The columns are equal, and (C) is correct.

18. C

The possible pitfall in this problem is misinterpreting the phrase "$\frac{2}{5}$ less than." This does not mean that James sold $\frac{2}{5}$ as many widgets as Steven; rather, it means that we need to subtract $\frac{2}{5}$ of the number Steven sold in order to find the number James sold. For example, if Steven sold 5, then James sold $5 - \frac{2}{5}(5) = 5 - 2 = 3$.

Let J be the number of widgets that James sold and let S be the number of widgets that Steven sold. The fact that the number of widgets that James sold was $\frac{2}{5}$ less than the number of widgets that Steven sold means that $J = S - \frac{2}{5}S$. So $J = S - \frac{2}{5}S = \frac{5}{5}S - \frac{2}{5}S = \frac{3}{5}S$. Thus, $J = \frac{3}{5}S$.

Since the total number sold is $J + S$, the fraction of the total sold in the previous week that were sold by Steven is $\dfrac{S}{J + S} = \dfrac{S}{\frac{3}{5}S + S} = \dfrac{S}{\left(\frac{8}{5}S\right)} = \dfrac{1}{\left(\frac{8}{5}\right)} = \dfrac{5}{8}$.

The quantities in the two columns are equal.

19. B

Here there are $\dfrac{1 \text{ inch}}{4 \text{ miles}} = \dfrac{1}{4}$ inches per mile.

In 28 miles, there are $\dfrac{1 \text{ inch}}{4 \text{ miles}} \times 28 \text{ miles} = 7 \text{ miles}$.

Column A is 7 and Column B is 8. Column B is greater and choice (B) is correct.

20. C

Since the carpenter earned $4j$ dollars for m hours of work, the carpenter was paid at a rate of $\dfrac{4j}{m}$ dollars per hour. Since the carpenter earned n dollars for $5w$ hours of work, the carpenter was paid at a rate of $\dfrac{n}{5w}$ dollars per hour. The carpenter is always paid at the same rate. So $\dfrac{4j}{m} = \dfrac{n}{5w}$. Cross-multiplying, we have $(4j)(5w) = (m)(n)$, so $20jw = mn$. The quantities in both columns are equal.

21. A

The average formula says that Average $= \dfrac{\text{Sum of the Terms}}{\text{Number of Terms}}$.

Since the average of x, y, and z is 12, $\dfrac{x + y + z}{3} = 12$.

Let's use this equation to find the value of $3(x + y + z)$.

Multiplying both sides of the equation $\dfrac{x + y + z}{3} = 12$ by 3, we have $x + y + z = 36$. Multiplying both sides of the equation $x + y + z = 36$ by 3 will give us $3(x + y + z) = 3(36)$, so we have $3(x + y + z) = 108$.

So in Column A we have $3(x + y + z) = 108$ and in Column B we have 72. 108 is greater than 72, so Column A is greater, and (A) is correct.

22. B

The decimal equivalent of 30% is 0.30, so Column A is $0.30 \times 18 = 0.54$.

The decimal equivalent of 40% is 0.40, so Column B is $0.40 \times 14 = 0.56$.

Column B is greater and choice (B) is correct.

23. C

The best way to approach this problem is to make the two columns look similar. This can be done by using the centered information to find a value for a.

First solve for b by replacing c with 15.

$$b = \frac{4(15)}{3} = \frac{60}{3} = 20$$

Then solve for a by replacing b with 20.

$$a = \frac{5b}{2} = \frac{5(20)}{2} = \frac{100}{2} = 50$$

Thus both columns are equal.

24. C

The simplest way to do this problem is to make the columns look similar without doing all of the math.

Since $32\% = \dfrac{32}{100}$, Column A can be re-written as $\left(\dfrac{32}{100}\right)(450)$.

Similarly, Column B can be re-written as $\left(\dfrac{64}{100}\right)(225)$.

We can multiply both columns by 100, leaving us with (32)(450) for Column A and (64)(225) for Column B.

Then, we can divide both columns by 32, leaving us with 450 for Column A and (2)(225) for Column B.

The final step is to simplify 2(225) for Column B.

(2)(225) = 550.

Since the quantities for both columns are equal, choice (C) is correct.

25. A

First, make Column A easier to deal with by determining the savings on each tape. The savings on each tape can be computed as Regular Price − Sale Price = 1.49 − 1.35 = 0.14. Since 15 tapes are purchased, the total savings will be (15 tapes)(0.14 per tape) = (15)(0.14).

Next, make the columns look similar by simplifying Column B.

$196 = 14^2$, therefore 1.96 = (14)(0.14).

Since both columns have (0.14) in common, we can remove it. This leaves us with 15 in Column A and 14 in Column B. Thus, Column A is greater.

If we didn't recognize that $196 = 14^2$, we could simply multiply (15)(0.14), and find that it is slightly larger than 1.96. An easy way to compute 15 x 0.14 is to write 15 as (10 + 5). Thus we have (10 + 5)(0.14) = 1.40 + 0.70 = 2.10, which is larger than 1.96.

26. C

This question relies on knowledge of right triangles. To get a better sense of the situation, we can draw a diagram.

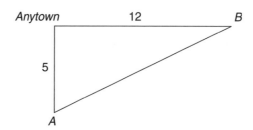

Since A is due south of Anytown and B is due east of Anytown, the lines that connect Anytown and A and Anytown and B form a right angle. Then, if we connect A and B, we have a right triangle. We know that the two legs of the triangle are 5 and 12 (these are the distances between Anytown and the 2 cities).

Now we can see that Column A refers to the hypotenuse of the triangle we drew. 5 and 12 are the two legs of a commonly tested Pythagorean triplet, 5:12:13. Because of this, we can be sure that the hypotenuse (the distance between A and B) is 13 miles. Therefore, the two columns are equal.

27. C

Column B looks much easier to evaluate. Given the perimeter and the fact that R is a square, we can calculate the area as follows. The perimeter of a square equals the sum of the 4 side lengths, or 4 x the side length. If the perimeter is 20, the side length must equal 5 since 4(side length) = 4(5) = 20. Now that we know the side length of the square, we can compute its area. The area of a square equals (side length)^2, so (side length)^2 = (5)^2 = 25. So, Column B is equivalent to 25.

We can now focus on Column A. The perimeter of a rectangle equals 2(length) + 2(width), so 2(length) + 2(width) = 20. Dividing both sides by 2, we see that the length + width = 10. So, whatever the dimensions of the rectangle in A are, we know that the length and the width must add up to 10.

Since the area of a rectangle equals (length) × (width), we can compute the area of the rectangle for different pairs of numbers that add up to 10. This will allow us to compare Columns A and B.

For example, suppose we try 1 and 9 for the length and width. This gives us an area of $1 \times 9 = 9$, so for these values A is less than B. We can also try sides of 3 and 7, which give us an area of 21; A is still less than B. If we try sides of 4 and 6, we get an area of 24. Notice that as the sides get closer together in size the greater the area becomes, but it always seems to be less than the 25 from Column B. In fact, only if we make both sides equal to 5 does the area equal 25 – and that makes R a square, as it is in Column B. Thus the largest value for R occurs when R is a square. Therefore the columns must be equal.

28. B

To make the columns look more alike, let's rewrite Column A by separating $\dfrac{100x^2 - 1}{100}$ into 2 fractions: $\dfrac{100x^2 - 1}{100} = \dfrac{100x^2}{100} - \dfrac{1}{100} = x^2 - \dfrac{1}{100}.$

Now they look more alike: Column A is $x^2 - \dfrac{1}{100}$ and Column B is x^2.

We can compare them piece by piece. Whatever the value of x^2 is, when we subtract $\dfrac{1}{100}$ from x^2, we will be left with less than x^2. So Column A is less than Column B.

CHAPTER EIGHT
Sentence Completions

SENTENCE COMPLETIONS QUIZ

Directions: Each of the following questions begins with a sentence that has either one or two blanks. The blanks indicate that a piece of the sentence is missing. Each sentence is followed by five answer choices that consist of words or phrases. Select the answer choice that best completes the sentence.

1. Although the research he cites is by now familiar to most scientists, the maverick physicist's own conclusions are completely _____.

    (A) boring

    (B) unexpected

    (C) consistent

    (D) prudent

    (E) perfect

2. If increases in production costs are _____ increases in output, then it is profitable to raise the output of a manufacturing plant.

    (A) no greater than

    (B) no less than

    (C) measured by

    (D) similar to

    (E) twice

3. Although most older workers are in agreement with the company's code of conduct, many younger employees find the code to be _____.

    (A) detailed

    (B) archaic

    (C) noteworthy

    (D) indubitable

    (E) empowering

4. Because it _____ more conditions than it _____, researchers ultimately rejected the new surgical technique.

    (A) exacerbated..palliated

    (B) intensified..magnified

    (C) mitigated..alleviated

    (D) cured..aggravated

    (E) improved..should

5. Prose that results from a stream-of-consciousness approach to writing may at times be interesting, but most works of any lasting value are the product of a _____ mental effort.

    (A) pretentious

    (B) meager

    (C) haphazard

    (D) focused

    (E) disconcerted

6. Because of her helpful, encouraging style, extensive knowledge, and _____ giving advice, her students viewed her not only as a teacher but also as a _____.

    (A) penchant for..a busybody

    (B) aversion to..a tormentor

    (C) knack for..a mentor

    (D) opposition to..a guru

    (E) talent for..an authoritarian

7. Much to their consternation, her opponents often took her lightly, not realizing that her _____ appearance _____ her prodigious skill on the tennis court.

    (A) artless..decreased

    (B) agile..heralded

    (C) ungainly..belied

    (D) gawky..precluded

    (E) athletic..gainsaid

8. Le Sueur's appeal is based more on the social _____ of her novels than on the _____ of her writing.

    (A) stigma..criticism

    (B) strata..inaccuracy

    (C) status..destruction

    (D) reform..legibility

    (E) relevance..style

9. Archaeologists and historians are in disagreement over the _____ of the _____; thus, the debate continues about whether or not it may be termed ancient.

    (A) origin..species

    (B) proposal..scientist

    (C) position..planet

    (D) merit..theory

    (E) age..relic

10. New evidence suggests that the studies conducted at the institute have been surprisingly _____, and that earlier criticism of those studies was based on _____ data and hearsay.

    (A) flawed..incomplete

    (B) outdated..convincing

    (C) accurate..erroneous

    (D) helpful..informative

    (E) challenging..missing

11. The laws and customs in that region are so uniformly _____ that even a visitor who travels through it briefly is expected to alter his or her behavior accordingly.

    (A) variegated

    (B) confusing

    (C) innovative

    (D) outmoded

    (E) enforced

12. Although the findings suggest a _____ between the two groups of subjects, no _____ relationship has yet been proven.

    (A) link..artificial

    (B) correlation..causal

    (C) contrast..familial

    (D) disparity..actual

    (E) disagreement..consensual

13. As the subject of a sentence, the use of the infinitive is not necessarily more _____ than the use of the gerund; often the choice is a matter of _____.

    (A) correct..taste

    (B) comprehensible..clarity

    (C) cogent..intelligence

    (D) comedic..speech

    (E) creative..originality

14. The recent storm was an _____ which surprised locals accustomed to the otherwise _____ placid weather.

    (A) anomaly..occasionally

    (B) augury..predictably

    (C) anathema..frighteningly

    (D) aberration..perennially

    (E) affront..uncomfortably

15. Possibilities that had been discounted by early researchers were later afforded a high degree of credibility when advances in technology made what had previously been _____ now highly _____.

    (A) benign..dangerous

    (B) revered..discounted

    (C) unthinkable..probable

    (D) uncharacteristic..pressing

    (E) unwarranted..presumptuous

16. Despite a steady _____ in productivity, revenue has decreased more rapidly, creating the need to reduce the size of the company's workforce.

    (A) goal

    (B) decline

    (C) flow

    (D) decrease

    (E) increase

17. Many of the earliest colonial houses that are still standing have been so modified and enlarged that the _____ design is no longer _____.

    (A) contemporary..applicable

    (B) original..necessary

    (C) miniscule..seen

    (D) initial..discernable

    (E) changed..apparent

18. The old man could not have been accused of _____ his affection; his conduct toward the child betrayed his _____ her.

    (A) withholding..dislike of

    (B) sparing..tolerance of

    (C) lavishing..antipathy of

    (D) promising..affection of

    (E) withdrawing..adoration of

19. Among the many _____ of the project, costliness cannot be numbered; the goals of the project's promoters can be achieved with impressive _____.

    (A) claims..alacrity

    (B) benefits..savings

    (C) efficiencies..highlights

    (D) features..economy

    (E) failures..innovation

20. A leading chemist believes that many scientists have difficulty with stereochemistry because much of the relevant nomenclature is _____, in that it combines concepts that should be kept _____.

    (A) imprecise..discrete

    (B) difficult..combined

    (C) subtle..diffuse

    (D) specialized..intact

    (E) descriptive..separate

21. When chemists tested the unknown liquid, they discovered that it was not inert, as they had originally suspected, but rather extremely _____.

    (A) unreactive

    (B) volatile

    (C) common

    (D) authentic

    (E) intrinsic

22. Robert Louis Stevenson's character Mr. Hyde was a true _____; his abhorrence of mankind was apparent in his every word and deed.

    (A) misanthrope

    (B) martinet

    (C) orator

    (D) progenitor

    (E) humanitarian

23. Scottish tartan weaving is a _____ craft; these handiworks must be faultless down to the last detail.

    (A) temperate

    (B) meticulous

    (C) obdurate

    (D) lucid

    (E) conspicuous

24. The mayor's speech was a harsh _____, condemning the police force for their failure to _____ the riot that had broken out in the town square.

    (A) tirade..vacillate

    (B) tedium..settle

    (C) aperture..mitigate

    (D) monotone..permeate

    (E) diatribe..quash

25. Many successful negotiators appear to be
    _____ but are actually shrewd and artful.

    (A) banal

    (B) ingenuous

    (C) obstinate

    (D) laconic

    (E) faithless

26. John Bayless _____ from Alcatraz Federal
    Penitentiary in 1941 only to be quickly
    _____.

    (A) escaped..assessed

    (B) exacerbated..removed

    (C) absconded..recaptured

    (D) cogitated..adopted

    (E) detonated..deceived

27. Studies indicate that only the most _____
    tasters can differentiate between brand name
    and generic colas.

    (A) motivated

    (B) equivocal

    (C) aberrant

    (D) discerning

    (E) compliant

28. Although the meeting place was meant to be
    _____, it soon became known to many
    people.

    (A) viable

    (B) destitute

    (C) morose

    (D) noxious

    (E) clandestine

29. The diplomats were expected to observe a
    _____ that forced them to bow or curtsey
    to foreign royalty.

    (A) solarium

    (B) protocol

    (C) wraith

    (D) mannerism

    (E) acumen

30. The convict pleaded with the parole board for
    an early release, saying that he had become a
    kind and decent man and had _____ his
    former devious ways.

    (A) recapitulated

    (B) rekindled

    (C) redacted

    (D) rebated

    (E) renounced

ANSWER KEY

1. B	16. E
2. A	17. D
3. B	18. E
4. A	19. D
5. D	20. A
6. C	21. B
7. C	22. A
8. E	23. B
9. E	24. E
10. C	25. B
11. E	26. C
12. B	27. D
13. A	28. E
14. D	29. B
15. C	30. E

SENTENCE COMPLETIONS
ANSWERS AND EXPLANATIONS

1. B

Our first step is to look for clues in the sentence about what sort of word we will need to fill in the gap. Because the sentence begins with "although," we can expect the latter part of the sentence to contrast with the first. Since the "research... is familiar," we should expect the conclusions to be the opposite of familiar – perhaps new, unfamiliar, or original. The fact that the physicist is described as a "maverick," or independent thinker, reinforces this prediction.

Choice (B) provides a good match for this prediction: *unexpected* conclusions contrast well with familiar research. Choices (A), *boring*, (C), *consistent*, and (D), *prudent*, do not provide any contrast with familiar. Choice (E) does not fit logically; there is no connection between whether the conclusions are *perfect* and whether the research is familiar or not.

2. A

The blank relates increases in costs to increases in output. But what kind of relationship are we looking for? Since we are told that it is profitable to raise output when this relationship holds, the cost increase is probably less than the increase in output. Which choice matches this prediction?

Choice (A) seems to work: *no greater than* is close to our prediction of less than. Let's examine the other choices to be sure that choice (A) is the best fit. *No less than* and *twice* would actually mean that costs went up MORE than output – that would not be profitable, so choices (B) and (E) are incorrect. *Measured by* and *similar to* don't indicate whether costs went up by more or less than output, so choices (C) and (D) don't make sense. Choice (A), *no greater than*, is, in fact, the best choice.

3. B

This sentence begins with a good clue: "although." This keyword tells us that whatever the older workers in the first part of the sentence think of the code of conduct, the younger employees in the second half are likely to feel very differently. The older workers are "in agreement with" the code of conduct. We can predict that the younger workers are in some way unhappy or displeased with the code.

Choice (A) doesn't make sense; the fact that the code is *detailed* isn't necessarily positive or negative. Choice (B) sounds better: *archaic* means outdated or no longer applicable – to be sure, a negative quality to the younger workers. Choice (B) seems to be a good choice, but let's check the others.

Noteworthy in choice (C), *indubitable*, or *unquestionable*, in choice (D), and *empowering* in choice (E) all say something good about the code. None of them provides the contrast with the older workers' attitude that we're looking for, so they don't make sense. Choice (B), *archaic*, is, in fact, correct.

4. A

The word "rejected" gives us a good clue about the overall meaning of the sentence. If researchers rejected the technique, there must have been something wrong with it. Notice that both blanks refer to the technique's effect on certain "conditions," with the word "more" indicating that the effect in the first blank was more common. Since we believe that the overall results of the technique were negative, the effect described by the first blank is probably negative.

Choices (A) and (B) are the only ones that offer negative words for the first blank; *exacerbated* means made worse and, in the context of medical conditions, *intensified* also means made worse. The other choices – *mitigated*, or moderated, in choice (C), *cured* in choice (D), and *improved* in choice (E) – are all positive relative to medical conditions, so they don't fit here.

Of choices (A) and (B), which is paired with a word that fits the second blank? *Palliated*, meaning improved or reduced the severity of, seems to make sense. Choice (C) would mean that the technique improved some conditions but not as many as it *exacerbated*; it would make sense that researchers would reject it. Choice (A) is correct. Note that in choice (B), the second word, *magnified,* would have a negative connotation, which would not make sense here.

5. D

The two parts of the sentence are connected by "but," indicating some kind of contrast. The first part refers to "stream-of-consciousness" writing, which is contrasted with "works of lasting value" in the second part. The term "stream -of-consciousness" implies unfocused, unselective mental effort, so we need a word that implies focused, selective mental effort on the part of the authors of "works of lasting value."

Choice (D), *focused*, meaning purposeful or attentive, works well – a *focused mental effort* is in clear contrast to "stream-of-consciousness." No other choice matches our prediction. Choice (C), *haphazard*, is, in fact, the opposite of what we need as is choice (E), *disconcerted*, or confused. Choice (A), *pretentious*, does not provide the needed contrast. Finally, we can eliminate choice (B) because a *meager*, or scanty, effort is unlikely to produce works of value.

6. C

Because the first part of the sentence discusses the teacher's positive aspects ("encouraging style" and "extensive knowledge"), the first blank probably adds another positive quality, and the second blank probably describes her as someone the students view favorably. Let's look for a match for the first blank.

A *knack for* or *talent for* giving advice is a desirable quality in a teacher, so choices (C) and (E) are definite possibilities. An *aversion to* or *opposition to* giving advice is not desirable, so we can reject choices (B) and (D). What about choice (A)? Having a *penchant for* means being strongly inclined to, but that does not mean that the advice is necessarily good or welcome. We can keep choice (A) around for now, but it seems less appropriate than choices (C) and (D). Now let's consider the second blank.

Being a *mentor*, or trusted advisor, is consistent with being helpful, having knowledge and giving good advice, so choice (C) seems good. What about choice (E)? Be careful here; an *authoritarian* is not someone who is wise or authoritative. Rather, it means someone who demands complete obedience. That's not how students are likely to view such a "helpful, encouraging" teacher, so we can reject choice (E). Likewise, *busybody* is not a positive term, so we can also eliminate choice (A). Choice (C) is correct; it makes clear sense when read back into the sentence:

Because of her helpful, encouraging style, extensive knowledge and knack for *giving advice, her students viewed her not only as a teacher but also as* a mentor.

7. C

Because her opponents took her lightly, we can infer that the first blank must describe her appearance in some negative way. For the second blank, we will need something to indicate that her negative appearance was actually masking her "prodigious" skill. Note that if you were not familiar with "prodigious," you could infer that, because her opponents regretted taking her lightly, it must mean that she in fact has considerable skill.

Let's start with the first blank. Eliminate *agile* in choice (B) and *athletic* in choice (E) because they describe her appearance in positive ways. *Ungainly* in choice (C) and *gawky* in choice (D) both mean awkward or uncoordinated, so they are good possibilities. Choice (A)'s *artless* can mean unskilled but more commonly means lacking in guile or cunning. We shouldn't eliminate it, but it seems less promising than *ungainly* and *gawky*, which are more directly related to poor athletic ability.

Let's look at the second blank for choices (A), (B), and (D). *Decreased* in choice (A) doesn't work; her appearance did not detract from her skill. *Belied*, meaning represented falsely, could make sense here, so keep choice (C). *Precluded*, meaning prevented, in choice (D) also doesn't work. So choice (C) is correct.

8. E

"More...than" tells us that the first blank will include a positive feature of writing more apparent in Le Sueur's writing than the positive feature of writing that fills the second blank. Let's start with the second blank. Because it is a lesser part of the author's appeal, we are looking for something normally positive about writing in general. We can eliminate the negatively charged *inaccuracy* in choice (B) and *destruction* in choice (C). Choice (D), *legibility*, does not fit; readers do not generally need to decipher an author's handwriting, so *legibility* does not factor into the author's appeal. So we are left with choice (A)'s *criticism* and choice (E)'s *style*, both of which are generally positive about an author's writing. As for the first blank, choice (A)'s *stigma* does not make sense; it is a negative term, not a likely basis for the appeal of Le Sueur's novels. On the other hand, choice (E)'s *relevance* fits well. The *relevance*, or applicability, of the novels to society could certainly be a more important feature of a work than the author's style.

9. E

The second clause tells us that the disagreement between the archaeologists and historians centers on the ancientness or age of something. Choice (E)'s *age* works in the first blank, and *relic* fits in the second blank. Let's take a quick look at the other answer choices just to be sure. *Origin* in choice (A) might work for the first blank, but *species* is not a good fit for the second blank. The origin of a species is something that would be debated by scientists, but not by archaeologists and historians. We can eliminate choices (B), (C), and (D), because a "scientist's proposal," a "planet's position," and a "theory's merit" are all unlikely to be ancient.

10. C

The sentence contrasts "new evidence" about the studies with "earlier criticism," so we can expect the blanks to have opposite charges. Let's start with the second blank, where the clues "criticism" and "hearsay" lead us to predict something negative. We can eliminate choice (B), *convincing*, and choice (D), *informative*. As for the first blank, we're looking for a positive word that contrasts with the second blank. We can eliminate choice (A), since *flawed* is negatively charged. Choice (E)'s *challenging* has a neutral charge, and does not contrast with *missing*. Choice (C) works well for both blanks: *accurate* contrasts strongly with *erroneous*.

11. E

The combination "so...that" indicates that the clause following "that" is the result of the clause preceding "that." The keyword "even" tells us further that this "result" clause continues and intensifies the meaning of the clause that contains the blank. We can predict the blank to be something that forces visitors to change. Choice (E), *enforced*, is an exact match for our prediction. The other answer choices don't work in this context. Visitors will not necessarily change their behavior because the laws and customs are *variegated* (multicolored or otherwise displaying variety), *confusing*, *innovative*, or *outmoded*.

12. B

The keyword "although" contrasts what the findings suggest about the relationship with what has yet to be proven. Let's start with the first blank, which we can predict to be a synonym of *relationship*. Choice (A), *link*, and choice (B), *correlation*, both are possibilities. We can eliminate the other three choices, which describe differences rather than relationships. What about the second blank? Choice (A) is not a good fit; an *artificial* relationship does not sound like much of a relationship, so "no *artificial* relationship" in the second clause does not contrast with a suggested *link* between the two groups in the first clause. Choice (B)'s *causal*, meaning "relating to cause and effect," works. The first clause says that the findings suggest a *correlation*; the second contrasts this by saying that no *causal* relationship has been proven. Test takers who read the answer choices too quickly might mistake *causal* for *casual* and incorrectly eliminate choice (B). Choice (B), however, works for both blanks and is the correct answer.

13. A

The sentence talks about the usage of grammatical entities, and says that no comparison can easily be drawn between two different kinds of usage. We can eliminate choice (B), which says that one usage is not more *comprehensible* than the other, but then says that the choice is often a matter of *clarity*. This answer contradicts itself. Similarly, choices (C) and (E) offer pairs of words that have similar meanings, and thus contradict each other in the context of the sentence. Choice (D) offers *comedic* for the first blank, which has nothing to do with grammar or with anything else mentioned in the sentence; this answer can be eliminated as well.

We are left with choice (A), which tells us that one usage is not more *correct* than the other, and that the choice is a matter of *taste*, or personal preference. This makes sense, and is the correct answer.

14. D

The fact that the locals are "surprised" by the storm is a clue to the meaning of the word that goes in the first blank. Choice (A), *anomaly*, and choice (D), *aberration*, both refer to a deviation from what is normal, and thus are good possibilities. The other choices for the first blank do not contain the element of surprise: choice (B)'s *augury* is an omen, choice (C)'s *anathema* is a curse or something hated, and choice (E)'s *affront* is an insult. What about the second blank? Choice (A)'s *occasionally* does not work; if the weather were only *occasionally* calm, the locals would not be surprised by a storm. Choice (D)'s *perennially*, meaning "year after year," fits well. Choice (D) is the correct answer.

15. C

The first part of the sentence tells us that things that had once been considered unlikely ("possibilities that had been discounted") were later considered very likely ("afforded a high degree of credibility"). This contrast is reflected in the part of the sentence containing the two blanks. So we can predict that the first word will be something meaning "unlikely" and the second will mean "likely." Choice (C) is a good match for our prediction: it tells us that what had previously been *unthinkable* was now highly *probable*. Let's check the other choices to be sure. Choice (A) offers a pair of contrasting words, but *benign* and *dangerous* have nothing to do with the context provided by the rest of the sentence. Choice (B) could work if *revered* and *discounted* were in the reverse order. We can eliminate choice (D) because *uncharacteristic* and *pressing* are not opposites. Choice (E) might be tempting; *unwarranted*, or groundless, works well for the first blank. But *presumptuous* does not work well for the second blank. It means "arrogant or excessively forward." It sounds a lot like *presumptive*, or probable, which would work here, so (E) is a trap for test-takers who confuse the two words.

16. E

The keyword "despite" contrasts what is happening to productivity with what is happening to revenue. Because revenue is decreasing, we can predict a word like meaning "increase" for the blank. Choice (E), *increase*, matches our prediction exactly. Let's take a look at the other answer choices to be sure. We can eliminate choice (B), *decline*, and choice (D), *decrease*; they describe the opposite of what we need here. Choice (A), *goal*, and choice (C), *flow*, don't work in this context because there is no contrast with the decrease in revenue. Choice (E) is the correct answer.

17. D

Let's start with the first blank. The clue words for the first blank are "modified" and "enlarged." Clearly, the design is no longer what it once was. So we need a word that describes the design *before* it was modified and enlarged. The only choices that fit this requirement are choice (B)'s *original* and choice (D)'s *initial*. Moving on to the second blank, we need a word that tells us that the original or initial design of the houses is no longer present or visible. Choice (D)'s *discernable* fits the bill. Choice (B)'s *necessary* does not.

18. E

The key to this question is in finding the answer choice that has the right form of agreement. The two blanks are related; we need to determine how. If the first blank contains a fairly positive word or phrase, such as *lavishing* or *being generous with*, then the second blank will contain a negative term, like *dislike of* or *hostility towards*. If the old man does *not* give a lot of affection, then his conduct toward the child will show his dislike.

There are no answer choices that fit this scenario, so it must be the other way around. The first blank requires a term that means something like *hiding* or *withholding*; the second must be filled with something like *love towards*. Only choice (E)'s *withdrawing* and *adoration of* show the correct agreement. The other answer choices do not show the requisite agreement.

19. D

The second blank is the easier of the two. We're told that the goals can be achieved with something "impressive;" so we are looking for a positive or at least a neutral word. And we need something that relates to "costliness." We're told in the first clause that costliness cannot be numbered among certain aspects of the project; it seems like we're being told that the project is not costly. So the "impressive" quality in the second blank will probably be something like *savings*.

We can eliminate choices (A), (C), and (E), since they don't offer anything appropriate for the second blank. Choices (B) and (D) both work. What about the first blank? Choice (B) suggests *benefits*, but this doesn't make much sense: why would "costliness" ever be considered a benefit? Choice (D) suggests the more neutral *features*. Reading the sentence with the words from (D) inserted, we're simply told that costliness is not a *feature* of the project, and that its goals can be achieved with impressive *economy*. The two clauses agree with and reinforce each other; this must be the right answer.

20. A

The second blank is where we will start. The scientists have difficulty because of what the nomenclature does: we can predict "that it combines concepts that should be kept *separated.*" Only choices (A), (D), and (E) offer words for the second blank that fit this prediction. For the first blank, we want a term with a negative charge, since most scientists have difficulty with the nomenclature it describes. Of the choices we have left, only (A) fits the bill, with *imprecise.* Choice (C)'s *subtle* is neutral, and choice (E)'s *descriptive* is positive. Reading back the sentence with choice (A) inserted confirms that this answer works.

21. B

We are looking for a word that describes the liquid. The keyword *but* tells us that the sentence contains a contrast — specifically, the word in the blank will contrast with *inert.* *Inert*, in this context, means "exhibiting no chemical activity; totally unreactive," so we are looking for a word that conveys the opposite idea—that the liquid was reactive. Choice (A) is the exact opposite of what we want. Choice (B) is correct: *volatile* means "highly changeable, explosive, or reactive." Choice (C) is incorrect; *common* may appear to contrast with the liquid's property of being *unknown*, but the contrast we are looking for involves the liquid's reactivity, and not the frequency with which it is encountered. (The scientists discovered that the liquid was not inert; they didn't discover that it was not unknown.) Similarly, we can eliminate choices (D) and (E) because *authentic,* meaning real or genuine, and *intrinsic*, meaning inner or inherent, do not involve the reactivity of the substance.

22. A

According to the sentence, Hyde's hatred of mankind was evident in all of his actions. Therefore the word in the blank that describes him must mean "people-hater." That is exactly what *misanthrope*, choice (A), means. If you were not sure of the exact definition, you may have still recognized the root *anthro-*, meaning "human," and the prefix *mis-*, which means "hatred." *Humanitarian*, (E), is the exact opposite of the correct answer. A *martinet*, (B), is a strict disciplinarian. An *orator*, (C), is a speaker, which doesn't have anything to do with hatred of humanity. Finally, (E), *progenitor* is an ancestor, in particular, a father, which is also irrelevant.

23. B

If the tartans are perfect down to the last detail, then the word in the blank must mean "characterized by extreme care for details." *Meticulous*, (B), means just that. *Temperate*,(A), which means "mild" or "moderate," has nothing to do with details, nor do (C), *obdurate*, meaning "hardened in feeling," (D), *lucid*, which means "clear," or (E), *conspicuous*, which means "clearly visible."

24. E

Let's start with the easier blank: the second. What would a mayor want the police to do about a riot? To put it down, of course. Choice (B), *settle*, and choice (E), *quash*, work well. Choice (C), *mitigate*, which means "to make less bad," is also a possible answer. Choice (D), *permeate*, meaning "penetrate," makes no sense, nor does choice (A), *vacillate*, meaning "to sway back and forth; hesitate." So, we are left with (B), (C), and (E). Going back to the first blank, we are looking for a means by which the mayor could condemn others, and we are left with (B), *tedium*, (E), *diatribe*, and (C), *aperture*. An aperture is an opening, which doesn't fit. Tedium is extreme boredom, which also does not make sense. That leaves diatribe, which means an abusive, condemnatory speech. Perfect. *Tirade* means basically the same thing, but was eliminated because of the second blank. *Monotone*, finally, is a lack of variation.

25. B

The structure of this sentence indicates contrast, indicated by the word "but." Since the negotiators are actually shrewd and artful, in contrast, they must appear to be the opposite. The word in the blank must therefore denote guilelessness or simplicity, which is exactly what *ingenuous*, (B), means. *Banal*, (A), means "predictable" or "trite," which is not the opposite of shrewd. *Obstinate*, (C), meaning "stubborn," *laconic*, (D), meaning "using few words," and *faithless,* (E), do not fit the bill either.

26. C

What would a person attempt to do from Alcatraz, a prison? Run away, of course! Choice (A), *escaped*, and choice (C), *absconded*, therefore, fit into the logic of the sentence perfectly. How about choice (B), *exacerbated*? That means "to make worse"—no good. Choice (D), *cogitated*, meaning "thought deeply," also does not work. *Detonated*, choice (E), meaning "set off an explosion," makes no sense either. Eliminate (B), (D), and (E). Let's take a look at the second blank now. "The prisoner ran away, only to be brought back right away," is a good paraphrase of the sentence. So, of *assessed*, meaning "analyzed" or "summed up," and *recaptured*, recaptured is definitely the better choice and (C) is correct.

27. D

This sentence suggests that only people who can sense very small differences can tell the difference between the generic and brand names. *Discerning*, (D), means just that. As for the other answer choices, motivation has nothing to do with the ability to tell the difference between two things. Neither does choice (B), *equivocal*, which means "undecided," nor choice (C), *aberrant*, meaning "deviant," nor choice (E), *compliant*, meaning "yielding."

28. E

The "although" in this sentence signals contrast. So we are contrasting "known to many people" to the word that should go in the blank. Our prediction should therefore be something like "secret" or "hidden," which is exactly what *clandestine*, choice (E), means. *Viable* means "workable." *Destitute* means "penniless." *Morose* means "extremely sad," and *noxious* means "offensive."

29. B

What is it that the diplomats are observing that forces them to bow or curtsey? Perhaps a rule or directive of some kind. The best fit here is choice (B), *protocol*, which means "a set of manners and or ceremony." Choice (D), *mannerism*, actually refers to a gesture or trait. A *wraith* is a ghost. A *solarium* is a glassed-in enclosure or room exposed to the sun, and *acumen* is sharpness in judgment.

30. E

If the convict has become kind and decent, he must have given up his former devious ways. The best fit here is *renounced*, choice (E), which means "given up, rejected, disowned." *Recapitulated*, choice (A), means "repeated or summarized;" this doesn't work. *Rekindled*, choice (B), means "relit, revived, or renewed;" this is the opposite of what the convict wanted the parole board to think. *Redacted*, choice (C), means "edited or revised;" this might seem tempting, but the word refers to documents, not to people. *Rebated*, choice (D), is a word that means "discounted" or "lowered," and refers to prices.

CHAPTER NINE

Analogies

ANALOGIES QUIZ

Directions: Select the pair of words that expresses a relationship most similar to a relationship expressed in the original pair of words.

1. LUMINARY : FAMOUS ::

    (A) picture : appealing

    (B) angle : acute

    (C) petition : lurid

    (D) corruption : political

    (E) figment : chimeric

2. HALE : HEALTH ::

    (A) ungenerous : review

    (B) cramped : style

    (C) revered : infamy

    (D) nervous : apprehension

    (E) dull : luster

3. DOVE : COVEY ::

    (A) cow : heifer

    (B) coven : witch

    (C) commoner : royal

    (D) whale : pod

    (E) lark : song

4. STARE : LOOK ::

    (A) peek : glare

    (B) want : crave

    (C) befriend : alienate

    (D) despair : worry

    (E) plan : escape

5. PIRATE : WAYLAY ::

    (A) couturier : deliver

    (B) drone : inspire

    (C) healer : ameliorate

    (D) student : compete

    (E) captain : sail

6. STARVE : SUSTENANCE ::

    (A) feign : pretense

    (B) abscond : cache

    (C) extemporize : rehearsal

    (D) stave : hunger

    (E) gamble : morals

7. INTER : OSSUARY ::

    (A) doubt : modicum

    (B) lodge : domicile

    (C) invoke : estuary

    (D) gambol : casino

    (E) shell : pod

8. QUERY : REJOINDER ::

   (A) provoke : reaction

   (B) distinguish : amalgamation

   (C) sequester : jury

   (D) edit : proviso

   (E) quell : rebellion

9. PANCREAS : ORGAN ::

   (A) knee : joint

   (B) stomach : obesity

   (C) artery : vein

   (D) tooth : molar

   (E) symptom : disease

10. LAUDABLE : PRAISE ::

    (A) painful : sympathy

    (B) flammable : warmth

    (C) newsworthy : attention

    (D) secondary : education

    (E) impossible : faith

11. ENUNCIATE : PRONOUNCE ::

    (A) recite : impress

    (B) reiterate : bother

    (C) inquire : ask

    (D) stop : cease

    (E) elaborate : explain

12. EFFULGENT : SHINE ::

    (A) vivacious : energy

    (B) ornate : wealth

    (C) intangible : substance

    (D) expensive : desire

    (E) humble : arrogance

13. GARRULOUS : TALK ::

    (A) lethargic : sleep

    (B) reticent : speak

    (C) religious : sing

    (D) boastful : brag

    (E) artistic : copy

14. TALON : EAGLE ::

    (A) fang : snake

    (B) hoof : cow

    (C) ink : squid

    (D) tusk : boar

    (E) claw : panther

15. ARTICULATE : CLEARLY ::

    (A) orate : impressively

    (B) shout : loudly

    (C) malign : incoherently

    (D) jest : stupidly

    (E) lecture : willfully

16. MISER : THRIFT ::

    (A) performer : artistry

    (B) politician : compromise

    (C) chauvinist : patriotism

    (D) jester : buffoonery

    (E) scientist : focus

17. WOUND : GORING ::

    (A) ponytail : braiding

    (B) furrow : plowing

    (C) tooth : brushing

    (D) fracture : casting

    (E) part : combing

18. SCRATCH : SCORING ::

    (A) sander : smoothing

    (B) hole : drilling

    (C) patch : strengthening

    (D) irritation : itching

    (E) loaf : slicing

19. CONJURE : SPIRITS ::

    (A) distill : beverages

    (B) incarcerate : prisoners

    (C) muster : troops

    (D) levy : taxes

    (E) uplift : moods

20. CHEEK : KOWTOW ::

    (A) face : insult

    (B) tongue : utter

    (C) candor : prevaricate

    (D) initiative : collaborate

    (E) parsimony : scrimp

21. LACQUER : FURNITURE ::

    (A) gloss : shine

    (B) mop : dirt

    (C) varnish : paint

    (D) polish : brush

    (E) wax : floor

22. MEANDER : WALK ::

    (A) prattle : talk

    (B) mutilate : destroy

    (C) legislate : mandate

    (D) draw : write

    (E) clamor : gather

23. QUATRAIN : SONNET ::

    (A) rhyme : poem

    (B) movement : symphony

    (C) appendix : textbook

    (D) plot : novel

    (E) clay : sculpture

24. ARSENAL : ARMAMENTS ::

    (A) hospital : surgery

    (B) airport : flights

    (C) pantry : foodstuffs

    (D) courthouse : justice

    (E) laboratory : experiments

25. WHET : APPETITE ::

    (A) revert : past

    (B) convene : group

    (C) pique : interest

    (D) expose : danger

    (E) solve : equation

26. SCRAWL : WRITE ::

    (A) induce : lead

    (B) mutter : speak

    (C) ascertain : verify

    (D) adjoin : contact

    (E) reclaim : demand

27. EWE : SHEEP ::

    (A) collie : dog

    (B) calf : cow

    (C) sow : pig

    (D) gander : goose

    (E) hatchling : egg

28. CARPENTER : SAW ::

    (A) teacher : chalk

    (B) accountant : calculator

    (C) chemist : beaker

    (D) knife : chef

    (E) surgeon : scalpel

29. LABORATORY : EXPERIMENT ::

    (A) zoo : concession

    (B) university : professor

    (C) courthouse : trial

    (D) gymnasium : medal

    (E) museum : foundation

30. DEBILITATE : WEAK ::

    (A) empower : strong

    (B) countermand : illegal

    (C) abominate : absent

    (D) instigate : guilty

    (E) retire : lifeless

ANSWER KEY ON FOLLOWING PAGE

ANSWER KEY

1. E	16. D
2. D	17. B
3. D	18. B
4. D	19. C
5. C	20. C
6. C	21. E
7. B	22. A
8. A	23. B
9. A	24. C
10. C	25. C
11. E	26. B
12. A	27. C
13. D	28. E
14. E	29. C
15. B	30. A

ANALOGIES
ANSWERS AND EXPLANATIONS

1. E

A LUMINARY is a brilliant or famous person. (The stem *lum-* means "light" or "bright.") Since the second word of the stem is FAMOUS, we know that the second meaning of LUMINARY is being used here, and the bridge is a characteristic one: a LUMINARY is characterized by being FAMOUS. Which choice has the same bridge? Choice (A)'s *picture* might be *appealing*, but the adjective is not a necessary characteristic; eliminate (A). Choice (B)'s *angle* need not be *acute*; it could be *obtuse*. Eliminate (B). Choice (C)'s *petition* need not be *lurid* ("horrific" or "sensationalized"); eliminate (C). Choice (D)'s *corruption*, though often found in politics, is not necessarily *political*. A *figment* ("a thing made up, or contrived") is characterized by being *chimeric* or fanciful; (E), therefore, is the correct choice.

2. D

HALE means "healthy." Someone who is HALE by definition has HEALTH. Which choice uses the same bridge? Someone who is *ungenerous* does not by definition have *review*, so eliminate (A). Someone who is *cramped* does not by definition have *style*: eliminate (B). Someone *revered* does not by definition have *infamy*; in fact, a *revered* person would never have *infamy* ("a bad reputation"): eliminate (C). Someone who is *nervous* or worried by definition has *apprehension*, or fear or unease over the future, so (D) is correct. Finally, something or someone *dull* lacks *luster*, rather than having it: eliminate (E).

3. D

This is a variation of a part/whole bridge: a group of DOVES is a COVEY. A *heifer* is a young *cow*, usually one who hasn't given birth. The bridge is wrong: eliminate choice (A). A *coven* is a group (or meeting) of *witches*, but the bridge is reversed: eliminate choice (B). A *commoner* is the opposite of a *royal*: eliminate choice (C). A group of *whales* is called a *pod*; therefore, choice (D) is the correct answer. Finally, a *lark* is a bird famous for its *song*; this is not the right bridge. Eliminate choice (E).

4. D

To STARE is to LOOK at intently or searchingly, so the relationship here is one of degree or intensity: to STARE is to look more penetratingly or intently. In choice (A), *peek* might be a less intense form of *glare*, but this is the reverse of the bridge we want. The same is true of choice (B); *wanting* is a lesser, not a greater, degree of *craving.* In choice (C), *befriend* is the opposite of *alienate*, not a more intense form of it. In choice (D), to *despair*, or to abandon all hope, is a more intense form of *worry*; this is the bridge we want. Choice (E)'s *plan* and *escape* have no special relationship. (D) remains the best answer.

5. C

WAYLAY means "to lie in wait for and attack; ambush." A PIRATE is one who, by definition, WAYLAYS. Which answer choice uses the same bridge? Choice (A) is a trap. A *couturier* is a clothing designer, not someone who *delivers*; but *couturier* looks a lot like *courier*, a word which does refer to someone who by definitions *delivers*. What about choice (B)? A *drone* is an insect who serves only in a reproductive capacity, or a person who does menial work. Neither, by definition, *inspires*. Let's looks at choice (C). To *ameliorate* means "to make better"; so a *healer*, by definition, does *ameliorate*. Hold on to (C). What about (D)? A *student* may or may not *compete*, but competing is not something that a student does by definition. As for choice (E), a ship *captain* may by definition *sail*, but an army captain or police captain does not. (C) remains the best answer choice.

6. C

To STARVE is to be deprived of SUSTENANCE (food, or that which sustains one). In choice (A), to *feign*, meaning "to pretend," is to use *pretense*. This is not the "lack bridge" we are looking for. In choice (B), a person can *abscond* (run off secretly into hiding) with a *cache* (a place for concealing goods, particularly valuables, or the goods kept there), but to *abscond* is not to be deprived of a *cache*. In choice (C), to *extemporize* is to do something on the spur of the moment without preparation; so we can say that to *extemporize* is to do without *rehearsal*. This choice looks very close to the stem. Choice (D)'s *stave* and *hunger* are often linked in the phrase *to stave off hunger*, but to *stave* is not to be deprived of *hunger* (actually, it means "to hold off or ward off"). As for choice (E), many people may think that gambling is immoral, but to *gamble* is not necessarily to be deprived of *morals*. Choice (C) remains the best answer.

7. B

To INTER (meaning "to bury a body or the remains of a body") is to put into an OSSUARY (a receptacle or resting place for the bones of the dead). To *doubt* does not mean "to place in a *modicum* (meaning "a little bit")," so eliminate choice (A). To *lodge* (it must be a verb here) means "to place someone temporarily in a *domicile* (dwelling place)." (B) is the correct choice. To *invoke* (call upon) does not mean "to place in an *estuary* (an inlet of the sea where salty and fresh water mix)." Eliminate choice (C). To *gambol*, not be confused with "gamble," is to frolic or dance about. *Gambol* does not mean "to place in a *casino*," so eliminate choice (D). To *shell* peas can mean "to remove them from a *pod*," but not "to place them in a pod." Eliminate choice (E).

8. A

To QUERY (ask a question) is to elicit a REJOINDER (answer). Likewise, to *provoke* is to elicit a *reaction*. Choice (A) has the same bridge as the stem, and is thus the correct answer. To *distinguish* is not to elicit an *amalgamation* (a combination or union of various things), so eliminate choice (B). Although a *jury* can be *sequestered* (put into seclusion), this doesn't resemble the bridge we're looking for, so eliminate choice (C). To *edit* is not to elicit a *proviso* (a clause in a contract or document providing a condition), so eliminate choice (D). Although a person can *quell* (put down) a *rebellion*, this is the opposite of eliciting a rebellion; eliminate choice (E).

9. A

A PANCREAS is, by definition, a type of ORGAN. Let's plug the choices into this bridge, and see which one fits. Choice (A) sounds good; a *knee* is a type of *joint*. Choice (B) doesn't work; the *stomach* is not a type of *obesity*. In choice (C), an *artery* and a *vein* are both types of blood vessels, but an *artery* is not a type of *vein*. Choice (D) uses the same bridge as the stem pair, but the words are in the wrong order. A *molar* certainly is a type of *tooth*, but a *tooth* is not a type of *molar*. Finally, in choice (E), a *symptom* is not a type of *disease*. Choice (A) is correct.

10. C

Because the second word in each of the answer choices is a noun, we can tell that PRAISE is being used as a noun. Thus, we can use a characteristic bridge to define the relationship between the adjective and noun in the stem pair: something LAUDABLE, by definition, is worthy of PRAISE. Choice (A) is incorrect because it contains a weak bridge; something *painful* is not necessarily worthy of *sympathy*. We can also eliminate choices (B) and (D) because it would not make sense to say that something *flammable* is worthy of *warmth* or that something *secondary* is worthy of *education*. Plugging our bridge into choice (E) also allows us to eliminate this word pair because something *impossible* is not defined as being worthy of *faith*. Choice (C) is the correct answer because something *newsworthy*, or of public interest, is by definition worthy of *attention*.

11. E

The stem pair have a degree bridge where ENUNCIATE, or articulate, means to PRONOUNCE more clearly and precisely. We can eliminate choices (A) and (B), because *recite* and *impress* have no definitive relationship, and *reiterate*, meaning "to repeat," has no necessary relationship with *bother*. Next, we can eliminate choices (C) and (D) because there is no degree difference between the words. In choice (C), to *inquire* means to *ask*, and in choice (D), *stop* has the same definition as *cease*. Choice (E) is the correct answer because to *elaborate*, which means to clarify or to discuss in depth, is, by definition, to *explain* something more clearly and precisely.

12. A

Our bridge for this stem pair is a characteristic bridge: something that is EFFULGENT, (meaning "bright or resplendent") is characterized by a lot of SHINE. Choice (A) uses the same bridge: something (or someone) that is *vivacious* is characterized by a lot of *energy*.

We can eliminate choice (B) because *ornate*, meaning "elaborate or heavily ornamented," does not have a necessary relationship with *wealth*. Likewise, we can eliminate choice (D) because *expensive* and *desire* do not have a definitive relationship. Recall that our correct answer must have a characteristic bridge. Choice (C) is incorrect because it has a lack bridge, the exact opposite of what we're looking for: something that is *intangible*, by definition, lacks *substance*. Choice (E) features another lack bridge: someone that is *humble*, by definition, lacks *arrogance*.

13. D

The adjective and verb in the stem pair clue us that we have a characteristic bridge: someone who is GARRULOUS, by definition, has a tendency to TALK a lot. First, we can eliminate any answer choices with the wrong bridge. Choice (B) is incorrect because it has a lack bridge: someone who is *reticent*, or reluctant to speak, by definition, does not *speak* much. Next, we can eliminate choice (E) because *artistic* and *copy* have no necessary relationship. We see that choice (A) is incorrect when we plug our bridge into this word pair because someone who is *lethargic*, or sluggish, does not necessarily *sleep* a lot. Likewise, choice (C) is also incorrect, because someone who is *religious* does not necessarily *sing* a lot. Our bridge only fits choice (D), because someone who is *boastful* is someone who has the tendency to *brag* a lot. Choice (D) is, therefore, the correct answer.

14. E

The bridge for this stem pair must be very specific. It's not enough to say that a TALON is part of an EAGLE's body; this bridge would work for choices (A), (B), (D), and (E). It's also not enough to say that a TALON is a body part used as a weapon by an EAGLE; this bridge works for choices (A), (D), and (E). Let's try a more specific version of the first bridge: a TALON is part of an EAGLE's foot. Unfortunately, that bridge still works for choices (B) and (E). We need to combine a couple of concepts here: a TALON is part of an EAGLE's foot that is used as a weapon. This function bridge works only with choice (E): a *claw* is part of a *panther*'s foot that is used as a weapon.

15. B

A characteristic bridge joins the stem pair: to ARTICULATE is to speak CLEARLY. The only answer choice that fits is choice (B): to *shout* is to speak *loudly*. While all of the answer choices have to do with verbal communication, only choice (B) fits into our bridge. Choices (A) and (D) have weak bridges: one may or may not *orate impressively*, and one may or may not *jest stupidly*. In choice (C), *malign* means to speak evil of someone; whether one does so *incoherently* is immaterial. Similarly, *willfully* does not characterize *lecture* in choice (E).

16. D

A characteristic bridge connects the stem pair: a MISER is characterized by THRIFT. The only answer choice that works with this bridge is choice (D): a *jester* is characterized by *buffoonery* or jests and pranks. For this question, it is important to remember that the bridge must by true by definition. For example, look at choice (A): a *performer* may have *artistry*, but not necessarily. Similarly in choices (B) and (E), a *politician* may or may not be characterized by *compromise*, and a *scientist* may or may not have *focus*. As for choice (C), a *chauvinist* is sometimes a person who is characterized by fanatical *patriotism*, but it can also describe someone who is intensely loyal to a gender, race, or other group.

17. B

By definition, GORING, or puncturing by piercing or stabbing, produces a WOUND. Choice (A) doesn't work: *braiding* produces a braid, not a *ponytail*. Choice (B) looks good: a *furrow* is, by definition, the result of *plowing*. Choice (C) doesn't work: *brushing* may clean a *tooth*, but it doesn't produce a *tooth*. Choices (D) and (E) have weak bridges: *casting* may immobilize a *fracture*, and *combing* may produce a *part*, but these relationships are not essential. Choice (B) is correct.

18. B

SCORING has several meanings. In this case there is a strong bridge that uses a less common meaning of the word: SCORING something, by definition, creates a mark or a SCRATCH. Choice (A) has a strong bridge: a *sander* is used for *smoothing*. But does *smoothing* something result in a *sander*? No. Choice (B) looks good: *drilling* something, by definition, results in a *hole*. The word pairs in choices (C), (D), and (E) don't display the same strong and necessary relationship found in the stem pair: *strengthening* does not necessarily create a *patch*, *itching* is more likely a result of, rather than a cause of, *irritation*, and *slicing* may be done to, but does not create, a *loaf*. None of these relationships is essential or similar to the bridge that relates SCRATCH and SCORING. Note that choice (D) is a same-subject trap for anyone who mistakenly interprets SCRATCH as a verb; however, the fact that *sander* can only be a noun makes it clear that the first term in each pair, including the stem pair, is a noun. Choice (B) is correct.

19. C

By definition, to CONJURE is to summon SPIRITS. We need a choice that uses the same bridge. Choices (A) and (E) are same-subject traps but lack strong bridges: *beverages* and *moods* are synonyms of other meanings of SPIRITS, which here refer to supernatural beings. Now look at choice (B). Does *incarcerate* mean to summon *prisoners*? No: *prisoners* are, by definition, *incarcerated*, but this is not the bridge we are looking for. Choice (C), however, is a perfect match: to *muster* is to summon *troops*. Choice (D) has a somewhat similar bridge, but there is a significant distinction between *levying*, or collecting, *taxes* and summoning ghosts or other SPIRITS.

20. C

This stem pair contains an example of an uncommon meaning of a common word. Someone with CHEEK, meaning boldness or impudence, does not KOWTOW or defer obsequiously. The same bridge appears in choice (C): someone with *candor* does not *prevaricate* or lie. Choices (A), *face*, and (B), *tongue*, are same-subject traps with the common meaning of CHEEK and can safely be eliminated. Choice (D) has a weak bridge since one may *collaborate* with or without *initiative*. Choice (E) has a strong bridge, but it is the opposite of the one we are looking for: someone who exhibits *parsimony*, meaning extreme frugality or stinginess, does, by definition, tend to *scrimp* or economize severely. Choice (C) is correct.

21. E

LACQUER is used to make FURNITURE shiny, the same way that *wax*, choice (E), is used to make a *floor* shiny. This is a function bridge. In choice (A), *gloss* is a synonym of shine; *gloss* is not used to make a *shine* shiny. A *mop*, choice (B), is a tool to clean away *dirt*—this is a function bridge, but a *mop* does not make *dirt* shiny. *Varnish*, choice (C), is not used to make *paint* shiny; like choice (A), *varnish* and *paint* are synonymous. *Polish*, choice (D), is applied with a *brush*; it is not used to make a *brush* shiny. So the correct answer remains choice (E).

22. A

To MEANDER is to WALK aimlessly or idly: this is a "type" bridge. Choice (A) has the same bridge—to *prattle* is to *talk* aimlessly or idly. To *mutilate*, choice (B), is pointedly to disfigure, that is, to *destroy* in a specific way, not to *destroy* aimlessly. To *legislate*, choice (C), may be to *mandate* through the creation of laws, but once again, there is no sense of idleness or aimlessness. To *draw*, choice (D), is certainly not to *write* aimlessly. Finally, to *clamor*, choice (E), is not to *gather* aimlessly; in fact, *clamor* and *gather* have no relationship at all.

23. B

A SONNET is composed of a group of QUATRAINs (more specifically, 3 quatrains and a couplet); this is a part/whole bridge. Is a *poem*, choice (A), composed of a group of *rhymes*? No: a poem may contain rhymes (though it doesn't have to), but it is not by definition composed *only* of rhymes. Is a *symphony*, choice (B), composed of a group of *movements*? Yes, it is. Is a *textbook*, choice (C), composed of a group of *appendices*? No: again, a textbook may contain appendices, but it is not composed solely of them. Is a *novel*, choice (D), composed of a group of *plots*? No. Is a *sculpture*, choice (E) composed of a group of *clays*? No, a sculpture may be made of clay, but it is not composed of a group of clays. So, the correct answer remains choice (B).

24. C

An ARSENAL is a place where ARMAMENTS are stored; this is a function/purpose bridge. Is a *hospital*, choice (A), a place where *surgery* is stored? No, a hospital is a place where surgery is performed. Is an *airport*, choice (B), a place where *flights* are stored? No. Is a *pantry*, choice (C), a place where *foodstuffs* are stored? Yes; this is the correct choice. Is a *courthouse*, choice (D), a place where *justice* is stored? No; justice may or may not be carried out in a courthouse, but it is not stored there. Is a *laboratory*, choice (E), a place where *experiments* are stored? No, experiments are conducted, not stored, in a laboratory.

25. C

To WHET is to stimulate APPETITE. Choice (C) has the same bridge—to *pique* is to stimulate *interest*. To *revert*, choice (A), is to return to an old habit, not to stimulate one's *past*. To *convene*, choice (B), is to meet, not to stimulate one's *group*. To *expose*, choice (D), may mean to lay open to *danger*, but it does not mean to stimulate danger. Finally, an *equation*, choice (E) may be *solved*, but to solve is not to stimulate an equation. Be careful of choices where the words are commonly used together. To whet the appetite is a common phrase, as is to revert to the past, to convene a group, to expose to danger, to pique interest, and to solve an occasion. But just because words commonly go together, they don't necessarily have the same bridge, as whet/appetite and pique/interest do. So, the best choice is (C).

26. B

To SCRAWL is to WRITE irregularly or in a way that is hard to understand; this is a type bridge. Does *induce*, choice (A), mean to lead irregularly or in a way that is hard to understand? No. Is to *mutter*, (B), to speak irregularly or in a way that is hard to understand? Yes. This choice looks pretty good; let's just make sure that the others are wrong. Choice (C)'s *ascertain* does mean *verify*, but not in an irregular or hard-to-understand manner. Choice (D)'s *adjoin* means that things are touching, but it does not mean to *contact*. And choice (E)'s *reclaim* does not mean to *demand* in an irregularly or hard-to-understand way.

27. C

A EWE is a female SHEEP; this is a type bridge. A *sow*, choice (C), is a female *pig*; this is the correct answer. As for the other choices, a *collie*, choice (A), is a breed of *dog*, not a female dog. A *calf*, choice (B), is a young *cow*, not a female cow. A *gander*, choice (D), is a male, not a female, *goose*. Finally, a *hatchling*, choice (E), comes from an *egg*, but it is not a female egg.

28. E

If we use the bridge "a CARPENTER uses a SAW", then any of the answer choices work. So we need a tighter bridge. What exactly does a carpenter use a saw for? For *cutting*. Does a *teacher*, choice (A), use *chalk* for cutting? No. Does an *accountant*, choice (B), use a *calculator* for cutting? No. Does a *chemist*, choice (C), use a *beaker* for cutting? No. Does a *knife*, choice (D), use a *chef* for cutting? No, a chef uses a knife—beware of reversed bridges like this one. Does a *surgeon*, choice (E), use a *scalpel* for cutting. Yes; (E) is correct.

29. C

A LABORATORY is a place where an EXPERIMENT is conducted; this is a function/purpose bridge. By the same token, a *courthouse*, choice (C), is a place where a *trial* is conducted. A *zoo*, choice (A), is not a place where a *concession* is conducted. A *university*, choice (B), is a place where a *professor* might work; not where he or she is conducted. A *gymnasium*, choice (D), is not a place where a *medal* is conducted, and a *museum*, choice (E), is not a place where a *foundation* is conducted.

30. A

To DEBILITATE means, by definition, "to make WEAK." By definition, to *empower*, choice (A), means "to make *strong*." To *countermand*, (B), by definition, does not mean "to make something *illegal*"; it means "to cancel or reverse an order." *Abominate*, choice (C), does not mean "to make *absent*"; it means "to hate." To *instigate*, choice (D), does not mean "to make *guilty*"; it means "to urge on." Finally, to *retire*, choice (E), does not mean "to make *lifeless*." Choice (A) remains the correct answer.

CHAPTER TEN

Antonyms

ANTONYMS QUIZ

Directions: Each of the following questions begins with a single word in capital letters. Five answer choices follow. Select the answer choice that has the most opposite meaning of the word in capital letters.

1. SURREPTITIOUS :

    (A) varied

    (B) clement

    (C) overt

    (D) magnanimous

    (E) feckless

2. DEMEAN :

    (A) feign

    (B) laud

    (C) lavish

    (D) inveigh

    (E) hemorrhage

3. CONTRITE :

    (A) impervious

    (B) unrepentant

    (C) legible

    (D) odious

    (E) original

4. ZENITH :

    (A) nuance

    (B) imprecation

    (C) finesse

    (D) dudgeon

    (E) nadir

5. VIGILANT :

    (A) enthralled

    (B) imprudent

    (C) momentous

    (D) oblivious

    (E) obtrusive

6. VALOROUS :

    (A) obsequious

    (B) wary

    (C) inexpensive

    (D) noble

    (E) cowardly

7. VERACIOUS :

    (A) reprehensible

    (B) pellucid

    (C) bogus

    (D) satiated

    (E) mundane

8. URBANE :

    (A) quiescent

    (B) rural

    (C) lithe

    (D) incendiary

    (E) unsophisticated

9. TRANQUIL :

    (A) insuperable

    (B) disconcerted

    (C) soluble

    (D) rooted

    (E) paltry

10. TEMPESTUOUS :

    (A) deft

    (B) repellent

    (C) cynical

    (D) placid

    (E) analogous

11. TORRID :

    (A) cool

    (B) unpleasant

    (C) cataclysmic

    (D) burly

    (E) fickle

12. ROTUND :

    (A) maudlin

    (B) lugubrious

    (C) intrepid

    (D) convenient

    (E) slender

13. SALIENT :

    (A) inconspicuous

    (B) fervid

    (C) imposing

    (D) lapidary

    (E) juvenile

14. RETARD :

    (A) legislate

    (B) jettison

    (C) gyrate

    (D) promote

    (E) founder

15. PROGENY :

    (A) grimace

    (B) ancestry

    (C) insurgence

    (D) millennium

    (E) ration

16. PLIANT :

    (A) acerbic

    (B) congenial

    (C) unyielding

    (D) fetid

    (E) punitive

17. INGRESS :

    (A) prowess

    (B) inclination

    (C) flora

    (D) gluttony

    (E) exit

18. INANE :

    (A) sensible

    (B) grubby

    (C) limpid

    (D) itinerant

    (E) prevalent

19. HYPERBOLE :

    (A) ramification

    (B) understatement

    (C) sobriquet

    (D) precision

    (E) inactivity

20. PRODIGAL :

    (A) frivolous

    (B) stupid

    (C) granular

    (D) thrifty

    (E) slipshod

21. GENUINE :

    (A) grievous

    (B) integral

    (C) laudable

    (D) spurious

    (E) obtuse

22. FLAMBOYANT :

    (A) reserved

    (B) onerous

    (C) primeval

    (D) rapacious

    (E) seraphic

23. EFFULGENT :

    (A) taciturn

    (B) wily

    (C) dull

    (D) empty

    (E) atrocious

24. MADDING :

   (A) easy to manage

   (B) unlikely to happen

   (C) marked by danger

   (D) full of anger

   (E) marked by quietude

25. FORMULAIC :

   (A) unusual

   (B) intuitive

   (C) predictable

   (D) formidable

   (E) unexceptional

26. CONSUMMATE :

   (A) amend

   (B) imitate

   (C) remain

   (D) initiate

   (E) complete

27. REGNANT :

   (A) submissive

   (B) repugnant

   (C) illegal

   (D) involuntary

   (E) supreme

28. VARIEGATED :

   (A) motley

   (B) irrigated

   (C) impossible

   (D) truthful

   (E) uniform

29. ORISON :

   (A) malison

   (B) sunrise

   (C) prayer

   (D) pause

   (E) disorder

30. PLENTEOUS :

   (A) ample

   (B) planted

   (C) agile

   (D) copious

   (E) scarce

ANSWER KEY ON FOLLOWING PAGE

ANSWER KEY

1. C	16. C
2. B	17. E
3. B	18. A
4. E	19. B
5. D	20. D
6. E	21. D
7. C	22. A
8. E	23. C
9. B	24. E
10. D	25. A
11. A	26. D
12. E	27. A
13. A	28. E
14. D	29. A
15. B	30. E

ANTONYMS
ANSWERS AND EXPLANATIONS

1. C

SURREPTITIOUS means "secret." The opposite, therefore, is "out in the open," which is the definition of *overt*, answer choice (C). Assuming that SURREPTITIOUS has something to do with repetition might have led to choice (A), *varied*, but that is an intentional trap set by the test maker. As for the other answer choices, *clement*, (B), means "merciful"; *magnanimous*, (D), means "generous"; and *feckless*, (E), is "purposeless," "ineffective," or "careless."

2. B

The prefix *de-* of DEMEAN usually suggests a negative word charge. In fact, to DEMEAN is to degrade, humiliate, or speak harshly to. Look for a word with a clear positive charge, meaning something like "to compliment or praise" or "to speak kindly to." Only *laud*, choice (B), and *lavish*, choice (C), have positive charges. To *laud* is to praise, which fits our prediction and is thus the correct answer. To *lavish* is to give generously; this is not the word we're looking for. To *feign*, choice (A), is to pretend or fake. To *inveigh*, choice (D), is to protest strongly against, and to *hemorrhage*, choice (E), is to bleed heavily.

3. B

CONTRITE means "deeply remorseful" (it's the adjective that gives rise to the noun *contrition*, meaning "remorse or repentance"). The opposite of remorseful is unremorseful, or *unrepentant*, which is choice (B). *Impervious*, choice (A), means "incapable of being penetrated"; *legible*, choice (C), means "readable"; and *odious*, choice (D), means "contemptible" or "hateful." Finally, choice (E), *original*, is the trap answer, because we might confuse CONTRITE with *trite*, which means "overused" or "hackneyed." The opposite of *trite* is "original," but that is not what we are looking for, so the correct answer is (B).

4. E

ZENITH means "the highest point." The antonym here will be a word meaning "the lowest point." Choice (E), *nadir*, means the lowest point; in astronomy, nadir is defined as the opposite of zenith. Therefore, choice (E) is the correct answer. A *nuance*, choice (A), is a shade of meaning; an *imprecation*, choice (B), is a curse; *finesse*, choice (C), is skillful, subtle handling of a situation; *dudgeon*, choice (D), is angry indignation.

5. D

VIGILANT means "watchful and aware." (Literally, it means "awake," "keeping *vigil* or watch.") The opposite of this would be a word meaning "unaware." *Oblivious*, choice (D), means just that, and is the correct answer. *Enthralled*, choice (A), means "captivated, entranced." *Imprudent*, choice (B), means "unwise," which is not the same thing as "unaware." *Momentous*, choice (C), means "extremely important." *Obtrusive*, choice (E), means "pushy" or "overly conspicuous."

6. E

The *val-* stem of VALOROUS appears in such words as "value," "valid," and "valiant," all of which are positive and have to do with strength. In fact, VALOROUS means "brave." If we didn't immediately know the meaning of the word, we could at least eliminate choice (D), the positively charged *noble*. In fact, *noble* can be a synonym of VALOROUS. *Obsequious*, choice (A), means "fawning" or "servile." *Wary*, choice (B), means "cautious." *Inexpensive*, choice (C), is a trap for anyone who may have mistakenly associated VALOROUS with valuable (*val-* is the stem of *value* but *valu-* is not the stem of *valorous*). Choice (E), *cowardly*, is the opposite of VALOROUS, and therefore the correct answer.

7. C

VERACIOUS means "authentic or truthful"; note the root *ver-* meaning "true" (found also in *verify*). The opposite of VERACIOUS is "untruthful." *Bogus*, choice (C), meaning "counterfeit" and, by extension, "false," fits perfectly as an opposite and is the correct choice. *Satiated*, choice (D) is a trap. It is very easy to confuse "veracious" with "voracious," which means "extremely hungry." *Reprehensible*, choice (A), means "blameworthy." *Pellucid*, choice (B), means "easily understood" or "transparent." *Mundane*, choice (E), means "common" or "everyday."

8. E

URBANE looks remarkably like *urban*, and for good reason: the words are related. URBANE originally meant "having city (as opposed to country) manners," but its modern meaning is "refined and sophisticated." The opposite of sophisticated is *unsophisticated*, which is choice (E), the correct answer. *Rural*, choice (B), is a trap for those who mix up URBANE and *urban*. *Quiescent*, choice (A), means "at rest." *Lithe*, choice (C), means "limber," or "moving easily." Finally, choice (D), *incendiary*, means "flammable," or "provocative."

9. B

TRANQUIL means "calm, composed, or undisturbed." The opposite would be a word meaning "agitated or disturbed." The word that matches our prediction is choice (B), *disconcerted. Insuperable*, choice (A), means "insurmountable." *Soluble*, choice (C), means "capable of being dissolved or solved." *Rooted*, choice (D), means "having a fixed position." Finally, choice (E), *paltry*, means "pitifully small" or "worthless."

10. D

TEMPESTUOUS is derived from the word *tempest*, and means "stormy." The opposite would be a word meaning something like "peaceful;" *placid*, choice (D), is a good fit and the correct answer. *Repellent*, choice (B), is a trap that the test maker has set for anyone who wrongly associates TEMPESTUOUS with *tempting*. In fact, the two have nothing to do with one another. *Deft*, choice (A), means "skilled," not "peaceful." Choice (C), *cynical*, meaning "distrustful of others' motives" or "pessimistically skeptical," and *analogous*, choice (E), meaning "comparable," have no connection with the stem or its antonym.

11. A

TORRID can mean either "extremely hot" or "extremely passionate" (think of the "TORRID zone," which is a warm area of the Earth, or "a TORRID love affair"). A good opposite, for both senses of the word, would be *cool*. This is choice (A), and is the correct answer. None of the other answers is related to the stem word. *Cataclysmic*, choice (C), means "catastrophic." *Burly*, choice (D), means "husky" or "stout." *Fickle*, choice (E), means "unreliable" or "changeable."

12. E

ROTUND means "fat," "round in shape," or "full in tone." Its stem *rot-* has to do with "round" and is the same stem as in *rot*ate (to go around). Once we have defined ROTUND, it is not very difficult to spot its opposite, which is *slender*—choice (E), the correct answer. Choice (A), *maudlin*, and choice (B), *lugubrious*, have roughly the same definition: "sentimental or sorrowful." Since they are so similar in meaning, they must both be wrong (because no test question can have two correct answers). *Intrepid*, choice (C), means "fearless." Choice (D), *convenient*, is unrelated to the stem word.

13. A

SALIENT means "conspicuous" or "sticking out" (think of the "SALIENT point" in an argument). The opposite of conspicuous would be *inconspicuous*, which happens to be choice (A). *Fervid*, choice (B), means "passionate." *Imposing*, choice (C), means "dignified" or "grand." *Lapidary*, choice (D), means "relating to precious stones." The correct answer is choice (A).

14. D

The verb RETARD means "to slow down" or "to hold back." (The stem *–tard* also appears in the word "tardy.") The opposite would be a word meaning "to speed up" or "to push ahead;" *promote*, choice (D), fits this prediction. To *legislate*, choice (A), is to make laws. To *jettison*, choice (B), is to cast off or throw overboard. To *gyrate*, choice (C), is to spin around. To *founder*, choice (E), is to sink or to collapse. So, the correct answer is (D).

15. B

The stem *-gen* is connected with "birth" (see *genesis* and *generate*), and the prefix *pro-* means "forth; forward." Thus, PROGENY is offspring—one's descendants taken as a group. Conversely, *ancestry*, choice (B), is one's ancestors or predecessors taken as a group. A *grimace*, choice (A), is a frown. An *insurgence*, choice (C), is a rebellion. A *millennium*, choice (D), is a period of one thousand years, and a *ration*, choice (E), is a portion or a share.

16. C

PLIANT means "flexible, bending, or compliant." The opposite would be a word meaning inflexible, unbending, or noncompliant. The best answer is choice (C)— *unyielding*. *Acerbic*, choice (A), means "bitter-tasting, or bitter in general" (as in *acerbic* humor). *Congenial*, choice (B), means "similar in taste or manner, in an agreeable way." *Fetid*, choice (D), means "rotten or foul." *Punitive*, (E), means "having to do with punishment."

17. E

The stem *-gress* is connected with "stepping" and "going." An INGRESS is an entrance; its opposite would be an *exit*, which is choice (E), the correct answer. *Prowess*, choice (A), is superior skill or strength. *Inclination*, choice (B), is a tendency towards something. *Flora*, choice (C), is plant life (as in "*flora* and fauna"). Finally, *gluttony*, choice (D), is eating to excess.

18. A

INANE means "silly" or "foolish;" its opposite would be a word meaning "serious." Choice (A), *sensible*, is the best match for this prediction. *Grubby*, choice (B), means "dirty." *Limpid*, choice (C), means "clear and simple" or "serene." *Itinerant*, choice (D), means "wandering." *Prevalent*, choice (E), means "widespread." Choice (A) is the correct answer.

19. B

HYPERBOLE means "exaggeration" or "overstatement." Even if we don't know the exact meaning of the word, the prefix *hyper-*, meaning "over," can help. Its opposite would be something like *understatement*, which is choice (B). *Inactivity*, choice (E), is a possible trap for anyone who associates "hyper" with hyperactivity. A *ramification*, choice (A), is a consequence. A *sobriquet*, choice (C), is a nickname. *Precision*, choice (D), is accuracy. Choice (B) is the correct answer.

20. D

Someone who is PRODIGAL is a big spender; the word means "wasteful with money." The opposite would be something like "frugal" or *thrifty*, choice (D). *Frivolous*, choice (A), means "petty." *Stupid*, choice (B), is a trap for those who might equate PRODIGAL with *prodigy*, an unusually talented person. The two words are actually unrelated, but sound alike. *Granular*, choice (C), means "having a grainy texture" (like *granulated* sugar). *Slipshod*, choice (E), means "carelessly done."

21. D

GENUINE means "real" or "authentic." The opposite would be a term meaning "false" or "counterfeit." Here, the stem word is well known, but the correct choice doesn't jump out immediately. Let's eliminate the words that we know don't work. *Grievous*, choice (A), means "causing grief," and *integral*, choice (B), means "crucial." These can be discarded. *Laudable*, choice (C), meaning "deserving of praise," doesn't seem to be connected with falsehood, and can also be thrown out. That leaves *spurious*, choice (D), meaning "inauthentic" or "counterfeit," and *obtuse*, choice (E), meaning "dull-witted" or "thick." Choice (D) is the best match for our prediction.

22. A

FLAMBOYANT means "showy" or "ostentatious," and is used to refer both to decoration and behavior. The opposite would be a word that means "understated" or "not showy." Choice (A), *reserved*, means "characterized by self-restraint or reticence," which fits our prediction. As for the other choices, *onerous*, (B), means "burdensome," *primeval*, (C), means "primitive" or "ancient," *rapacious*, (D), means "greedy" or "grasping," and *seraphic*, (E), means "angelic." None of these is related to the stem word.

23. C

EFFULGENT means "bright" or "shining," so its opposite would be a word like *dull*—choice (C). The stem word has nothing to do with the quality of being full, so *empty*, choice (D), is a trap. As for the other choices, *taciturn*, (A), means "silent"; *wily*, (B), means "crafty"; and *atrocious*, (E), means "wickedly horrible." All are unrelated.

24. E

MADDING is in fact related to "mad," but we must make sure we have the correct meaning of "mad." MADDING is derived from the meaning "crazy, wild, or insane" (like a "madman"), rather than "angry;" it means "frenzied" or "raging, furious." Don't confuse it with *maddening*, which means "driving someone crazy." The only answer choice here involving anger, (D), would be a synonym (no part of MADDING suggests the opposite of anger), so it can be eliminated. Choices (B) and (C) can also be ruled out because they are unconnected with MADDING. Choice (A) might be tempting, because something frenzied, raging, or furious would be difficult to manage, but "difficult to manage" is not the definition of MADDING, so *easy to manage* is not a good antonym. The opposite of "frenzied" or "raging" would be "calm," and answer (E), *marked by quietude*, is the best match. (Note that "quietude" is "calmness," not necessarily "silence.")

25. A

The word FORMULAIC has as its root "formula." Something FORMULAIC goes according to formula and is, therefore, routine and predictable. Eliminate choices (C) and (E) as synonyms. The opposite of routine and predictable would be *unusual*, so choice (A) is the credited answer. Choice (B), *intuitive*, means "knowing or known instinctively" and has nothing to do with FORMULAIC. Choice (D), *formidable*, meaning "difficult" or "inspiring fear or awe" is also unrelated to FORMULAIC.

26. D

CONSUMMATE is made up of the root *-sum-*, which, just like in math, means "total," and the prefix *con-*, which means "with" or "together." Now look at the answer choices: they are all verbs. Thus, even if we don't know exactly what CONSUMMATE means, we can guess that it's a verb meaning something like "bring to a sum total." Its precise meaning is "to complete" or "to fulfill." A good antonym for a word meaning "to complete" would be a word meaning "to begin;" therefore, choice (D), *initiate*, is the credited answer. Choice (A), *amend*, means "to correct or revise," and is unrelated to the stem word. Choices (B) and (C) are also unrelated. Choice (E) is a synonym.

27. A

REGNANT means "reigning, ruling, having authority, prevalent, or dominant." It looks very much like the word "reign," and in fact both come from the same Latin root. We can predict that the opposite will mean "subordinate," "submissive," or "powerless." Choice (A), *submissive*, is the credited choice. Choices (B), *repugnant*, which means "disgusting," (C), *illegal*, and (D), *involuntary*, are unconnected with the meaning of this word. Choice (E), *supreme*, is a synonym.

28. E

The word VARIEGATED contains the stem *vari-*, also found in words like "variable" and "vary;" all these words have to do with "difference" Specifically, VARIEGATED has to do with outward appearance, and means "marked with various colors" or "varied." Choice (A), *motley*, is a synonym. Choices (B), *irrigated*, (C), *impossible*, and (D), *truthful*, are all unrelated to the stem word. Only choice (E), *uniform*, works as an opposite.

29. A

The word ORISON contains the root *or-*, having to do with the mouth or speech; it is also seen in such words as "oral," and "oration." An ORISON, in fact, is a prayer. Knowing this, we can instantly eliminate choice (C) as a synonym. The credited answer is choice (A), *malison*, meaning "a curse." Choices (B), (D) and (E) are wholly unrelated.

30. E

PLENTEOUS shares the same root as the word "plenty," and means "abundant, copious." Choice (E), *scarce*, is, therefore, the credited answer. Choice (A), *ample*, and choice (D), *copious*, are synonyms of the stem word, and of each other. Choices (B) and (C) are unrelated to the stem word.

CHAPTER ELEVEN

Reading Comprehension

READING COMPREHENSION QUIZ

Directions: Answer each question based on what is stated or implied in the passage preceding the question.

To all appearances, the novelist Henry James and the philosopher William James, though brothers, seem to have had very little in
Line common, either personally or creatively. From
5 their unconventional early upbringing, they differed in almost every measure of disposition, temperament, and philosophy. Yet a closer analysis of their work reveals that they did share several intellectual traits and concerns.

10 Preferring to play the role of the observer, Henry James lived a life of contemplation, in the belief that ideas had value apart from any action they might lead to. Henry developed his novels through quiet reflection upon his own
15 circumstance as an American expatriate in Europe. Thus, in describing the intimate, personal thoughts and details of his characters, he also revealed his own. He was fascinated, nevertheless, by social interaction, especially
20 social and cultural restrictions on the individual. One sees this interest in society throughout his novels in the cultural clash between American outsiders and upper class Europeans, particularly in such works as <u>Daisy</u>
25 <u>Miller</u> and <u>Portrait of a Lady</u>.

While Henry was sometimes criticized for writing ponderous works that focused too narrowly on the inner lives of his characters, his brother William was preoccupied with
30 humanity's freedom to act, and all the ramifications thereof. His groundbreaking work in psychology emphasized a material and biological root to mental activity over the traditional view of his day: consciousness,
35 which held primacy in his brother's work, was

for William only the subjective experience of the physical activities of the brain. When William expanded his research into questions of religion and philosophy, he developed the
40 theory later called Pragmatism, in which the truth of any belief or value was inseparable from its practical consequences.

Despite their vast differences, both Henry and William James predicated their worldviews
45 on reason over faith and tradition, leading them to reject, for example, previously accepted notions of the impetus to action. Each independently formulated the notion of the "stream of consciousness," now taken for
50 granted: that the mind is not an orderly chamber through which thoughts march in linear fashion, presided over by reason, as was generally believed, but rather, that thought proceeds in a constant, disorderly manner from
55 the experiences, perceptions, and emotions of the individual.

1. The author's primary purpose in this passage is to:

   (A) Dispute the views of most writers who see William and Henry James as intellectual equals.

   (B) Evaluate the comparative contributions of William and Henry James to intellectual history.

   (C) Discuss the common intellectual ground the Jameses shared despite appearances to the contrary.

   (D) Argue that the ideas of Henry and William James should be evaluated according to the different standards of their disciplines.

   (E) Discuss how the contemplative, expatriate lifestyle of the James brothers independently resulted in their intellectual similarities.

2. Based on the ideas contained in the passage, the fact that Henry and William independently arrived at the notion of the "stream of consciousness" suggests that:

   (A) Neither of the men took seriously the ideas of the other.

   (B) Reason played little part in their thought processes, despite their intelligence.

   (C) The James brothers were unusual in that their minds processed ideas in orderly, linear ways.

   (D) Some aspect of their intellectual background led each of them to reach the same conclusion.

   (E) They must have had some intellectual correspondence or communication that biographers have overlooked.

3. If the author is correct in his assessment, Henry James would most likely have agreed with all of the following ideas EXCEPT:

   (A) An American of James's day would have had trouble fitting into upper class European society.

   (B) An individual's identity is based on his perceptions, experiences, and feelings.

   (C) The most productive way to gain knowledge is through methodical analysis of material causes.

   (D) Even ideas that are impractical can be important.

   (E) Individuals inhabit and interact with a context of cultural and social influences.

4. Which of the following best expresses the author's view of the relationship between literature and scientific research?

   (A) Literature and science cannot be compared because they inevitably are concerned with completely different kinds of knowledge.

   (B) Literary works reveal more about their authors than scientific works do.

   (C) Literature and scientific research can each reflect personal concerns.

   (D) Literature and science are ultimately different branches of the same approach to knowledge.

   (E) Literature and science should both emphasize reason and fact over tradition and belief.

5. Which of the following statements best describes William James's attitude toward religion, as expressed in the passage?

   (A) The existence of God cannot be proven, so it must not be true.

   (B) A religious belief is beneficial if it leads its followers to live moral lives.

   (C) All legitimate religions can have their practices validated by scientific inquiry.

   (D) Philosophical inquiry is a better method for exploring religious ideas than literature.

   (E) Religious ideas have value in and of themselves, whether or not they lead to action.

6. Based on the passage, which of the following was most probably the point of Henry James's exploration of "the cultural clash between American outsiders and upper-class European society"?

   (A) To demonstrate that Americans could easily assimilate into European society.

   (B) To show that, because of differences in upbringing, Americans would have been limited in their social interactions in European society.

   (C) To argue in favor of more understanding between people of different cultures.

   (D) To reveal that expatriate Americans in Europe would have been limited to the role of observers of society in their adopted homes.

   (E) To show that contemplative exploration of cultural tensions reveals an author's consciousness.

Why do we read biographies of famous
philosophers? It is hardly their lives or their
actions that make them important. Unlike a
Line statesman or a general, a philosopher becomes
5 distinguished by his or her writing and
thinking. Mill wrote an autobiography that still
merits attention today, but only because of the
heavily philosophical content of the book.
Perhaps this question is never more pertinent
10 than when considering the case of Hegel. Terry
Pinkard's recent book, *Hegel: A Biography*,
attempts to shed light on a man who has been,
for nearly two centuries, hidden behind his
writings. But while the reader learns much
15 from this book about Hegel the man, in the end
the question remains: why bother?

Even more than other philosophers,
Hegel hardly seems human. Beyond his
boyhood, he had no functioning first name;
20 even his wife called him "Hegel." Anthony
Quinton, a modern-day Hegel scholar, refers to
Hegel's "singularly abstract transcendence" to
illustrate his distance from more easily
humanized subjects. Before Pinkard's work,
25 Hegel did not have a modern, scholarly
biographer; perhaps would-be writers decided
that there was no subject worth examining
behind the philosophy and that further analysis
of his difficult theoretical texts was sufficient.

30 Before taking on the philosopher's life,
Pinkard wrote a book about Hegel's
Phenomenology; he understands that the role of
a work like his biography is secondary to the
more substantive concerns of philosophy itself.
35 His book attempts to provide context, both
personal and political, for Hegel's theoretical
work and succeeds at this limited goal.
However, Pinkard never satisfactorily answers
the burning question: why read about what he
40 did when we care about what he thought? As
Quinton claims, Hegel did transcend time and
place in his writings. Of course, were Hegel

transplanted to twenty-first-century America,
he might write different things, but the political
45 and social world of Germany in 1800 is only
superficially relevant to any reader seeking a
deep understanding of Hegel's thought.
Ultimately, because Pinkard does not explain
why we should care about his subject, he leaves
50 us wondering what compelled us to wonder
about the subject at all.

7. The author refers to Mill in order to suggest
that:

(A) Had Hegel written an autobiography, it
might have been worth reading.

(B) Mill satisfactorily answers the question
posed at the beginning of the passage.

(C) Successful philosopher biographies do not
focus on the life of the subject as much as
they focus on the philosophy of the
subject.

(D) Mill was more of a statesman or general
than a philosopher.

(E) Pinkard should have focused more heavily
on Hegel's philosophy.

8. According to the passage, Hegel is thought of as less human than other philosophers because

    I.   he was unique in the degree to which his thought transcended the everyday

    II. he focused on areas of philosophy approached only by the greatest minds in his field

    III. no one called him by his first name

    (A) I only

    (B) II only

    (C) III only

    (D) I and II only

    (E) I and III only

9. The author states all of the following about Pinkard EXCEPT:

    (A) He understands the role of philosopher biography.

    (B) His writing is heavily theoretical and abstract.

    (C) His biography is not the only thing he has written about Hegel.

    (D) He provides political context for Hegel's thought.

    (E) He fails to effectively explain the usefulness of philosopher biography.

10. It can be inferred that the author views philosopher biographies as

    (A) less useful than works about a philosopher's thinking and writing.

    (B) less interesting than biographies of statesmen and generals.

    (C) less satisfying than philosopher autobiographies.

    (D) less informative than Mill's autobiography.

    (E) less pertinent than books about the political and social context in which philosophers wrote.

11. The author's primary purpose is to:

    (A) Resolve the question of what the focus of a philosopher biography should be.

    (B) Persuade the reader to read Hegel's writing instead of writings about Hegel.

    (C) Defend Pinkard's book against charges of irrelevance.

    (D) Question the usefulness of one example of philosopher biography.

    (E) Explain the problems of writing a biography of an enigma like Hegel.

12. Which of the following best describes the relationship of the second paragraph to the passage as a whole?

    (A) It explains the characteristics of all philosophers so that the author can make generalizations in the final paragraph.

    (B) It asserts that Hegel is an exception among philosophers in order to avoid discussing Hegel or his biographers.

    (C) It defends Hegel against charges of inhumanity so that the reader will have an accurate view of his place in the history of philosophy.

    (D) It suggests that Hegel's "singularity" makes it impossible to successfully write about him.

    (E) It provides background information about Hegel so that the reader can better understand the argument that follows.

13. Which of the following phrases best captures the meaning of the expression "easily humanized" in the second paragraph of the passage?

    (A) malleable under the influence of philosophical mentors

    (B) simple and straightforward in social matters

    (C) readily brought to life for modern-day readers

    (D) effortlessly researched and understood by modern-day biographers

    (E) politically forward-looking

ANSWER KEY ON FOLLOWING PAGE

ANSWER KEY

1. C

2. D

3. C

4. C

5. B

6. B

7. C

8. E

9. B

10. A

11. D

12. E

13. C

READING COMPREHENSION
ANSWERS AND EXPLANATIONS

Passage Analysis:

Topic: Henry and William James

Scope: The similarity in the brothers' approach to consciousness and mental activity

Purpose: To describe how Henry and William James' work, though seemingly very different, shared certain psychological interests.

Paragraph 1: Henry and William James, though seemingly very different, shared "several intellectual traits and interests."

Paragraph 2: Henry James's life of contemplation and use of his own experiences in his novels. How his literary works show his interest in social interaction.

Paragraph 3: William James's psychological work. His belief that consciousness is material and biological. He develops this notion into Pragmatism.

Paragraph 4: Similarity of both brothers' worldviews: reason over faith and tradition. Two examples of conclusions they both reached.

1. C

This *global* question asks for the author's primary purpose. In this passage, the first paragraph stands as a statement of the purpose; the first sentence, begins "to all appearances," implying that what follows—a statement of the perceived differences between the James brothers personally and creatively—is somehow concealing the opposite, in this case, similarity, which is suggested by the word "share" in the last sentence of this paragraph. This is exactly what choice (C), the credited answer, says.

Choice (A) is wrong because the passage does not dispute whether or not the James brothers were intellectual equals. Choices (B) and (D) are both out, because the passage never tries to evaluate either brother's ideas; it only describes them. Choice (E) is a distortion; only Henry James was a contemplative expatriate.

2. D

The word "suggests" means that this is an *inference* question. We are asked to draw a conclusion based on the passage, about the fact that the James brothers independently arrived at the notion of "stream of consciousness." This idea is mentioned in the second sentence of paragraph 4. But also note the context: the previous sentence suggests a similarity between the brothers—their reliance on reason over faith and tradition in developing their worldviews—and continues with an example of how this led them both to the same conclusion. The "stream of consciousness" sentence is a second example of their both reaching the same conclusion. Choice (D) describes this, and so is correct.

Choices (A) and (E) are outside the scope of the passage. Choice (B) is a 180; as stated above, the passage says that they both relied on reason. Choice (C) distorts a line from the passage.

3. C

This is an *inference* question; the word EXCEPT tells us that the credited answer will be the only one that is *not* supported in the passage. Choice (A) paraphrases the last sentence of paragraph 2. The evidence for choice (B) can be found in paragraph 2, sentence 3, which focuses on James's interest in describing his novels' characters intimate, personal thoughts, and in the first sentence of paragraph 3, which says that Henry James was "criticized for writing ponderous works that focused...on the inner lives of his characters"; in other words, he described his characters' individual identities by showing their perceptions, experiences, and feelings. Choice (C) describes William's, but not Henry's, approach to life as described in paragraph 3: an emphasis on "a material and biological root of mental activity," and his development of the theory of Pragmatism. (C) is thus the credited answer. Choice (D) paraphrases the first sentence of paragraph 2 ("ideas had value apart from any action they might lead to") and choice (E) paraphrases paragraph 2, sentence 4 (fascination with "social interaction, especially social and cultural restrictions on the individual.").

4. C

This is an *inference* question that asks us to draw a general conclusion based on the passage. The passage discusses how Henry and William James had similar worldviews, and applied them to their different disciplines, Henry to literature and William to science. The author certainly would agree that Henry and William each applied their personal concerns to their work. Thus choice (C) is a valid inference, and is the credited answer.

Choice (A) is a 180; as stated above, the author does find them comparable. Choice (B) is a comparison that is not supported by anything that the passage says, and thus is out of scope. Choice (D) is too extreme. The author suggests that the James brothers each approached their disciplines from a similar intellectual background, but he does not imply that the disciplines themselves have the same basis. Choice (E) is the "is/ought" trap: the author says that the James brothers did emphasize reason over faith and tradition, but does not recommend that the disciplines *should* do so.

5. B

This is an *inference* question, requiring us to evaluate which answer choice is best supported by what the passage says about William James' views on religion. Note especially the last sentence of paragraph 3: "When William expanded his research into questions of religion and philosophy, he developed the theory later called Pragmatism, in which the truth of any belief or value was inseparable from its practical consequences." This idea—that a belief that results in good consequences must be good—provides strong support for choice (B).

There is little support in the passage for choices (A) or (C). Choice (D) is out of scope; William James's opinion of literature is not discussed in the passage at all. Choice (E) is a distortion of the passage; it was Henry James who believed that ideas have value in and of themselves.

6. B

To answer this *inference* question, we'll first need to look at the relevant quote (in the last sentence of paragraph 4) and its immediate context. The previous sentence mentions James's fascination with "social interaction, especially social and cultural restrictions on the individual." So the "cultural clash" described by the sentence quoted above is probably a demonstration of social and cultural restrictions on the individual. Choice (B) puts this all together, suggesting that differences in social backgrounds would create limits for Americans in European society. So (B) is the credited answer.

Choice (A) is the exact opposite of what the passage tells us. Choice (C) is out of scope: we are never told that Henry James argued for more cross-cultural understanding. Choice (D) distorts information from various parts of the paragraph: sentence 1 calls James an "observer"; sentence 2 calls him an "American expatriate." But these descriptions of James are not connected with the "cultural clash" mentioned in the last sentence. Choice (E) might be something that the passage's author would suggest about Henry James, but we don't know that James himself would suggest it.

Passage Analysis:

Topic: Biographies of philosophers

Scope: Pinkard's recent biography of Hegel

Purpose: To criticize Pinkard's book and to question the importance of philosopher biographies in general

Paragraph 1: Frames a broad question regarding the biographies of philosophers, and narrows the focus to a recent biography of Hegel

Paragraph 2: Illustrates why Hegel's case is particularly useful for this discussion

Paragraph 3: Criticizes the biographer because he did not answer the question posed at the beginning of the passage

7. C

By referring to Mill, the author illustrates his point that a book focusing on a philosopher's life is less interesting than one focusing on the philosopher's thoughts. Mill's autobiography is given as an example of the latter, as choice (C) indicates.

Let's check the other answer choices. Choice (A) is incorrect because the possibilities of an autobiography by Hegel are outside the scope of the passage. Choice (B) is incorrect because the author does not tell us if, or how, Mill would answer this question. Choice (D) is incorrect because Mill was, in fact, a philosopher and because it is outside the scope of the remark the question refers to. Choice (E) is incorrect because, while the author might endorse this idea, the comments about Mill's autobiography are not made for the purpose of suggesting improvements to Pinkard's work. Choice (C) is the credited answer.

8. E

Statement I is true: Quinton refers to Hegel's transcendence as "singularly abstract." Eliminate choices (B) and (C). Statement II is outside the scope of the passage. Eliminate choice (D). Statement III is confirmed by lines 18-20. Eliminate choice (A). Statements I and III both come from material in the passage and are directly relevant to the question. Choice (E) is the credited answer choice.

9. B

In this *detail* question, our task is to find support in the passage for four of the answers and to eliminate them. The one answer that does not have textual support is the right choice. Choice (A) is incorrect because the author does credit Pinkard for understanding his role in providing context (paragraph 3, sentence 1). Choice (C) is incorrect because the author refers to another book about Hegel by Pinkard (paragraph 3, sentence 1). Choice (D) is incorrect because the author explains that Pinkard does provide political context (paragraph 3, sentence 2). Choice (E) is incorrect because it, in fact, summarizes the author's main complaint about Pinkard's approach (paragraph 3, sentence 6). Hegel's writing is "theoretical" (paragraph 2, sentence 4) and "abstract" (paragraph 2, sentence 3), not Pinkard's. We learn nothing of Pinkard's prose style. Thus, choice (B) is correct.

10. A

The two rhetorical questions that the author uses to frame the first paragraph deal with the usefulness of philosopher biographies. Such works are contrasted with Mill's autobiography, which focuses heavily on his ideas (paragraph 1, sentence 3), as well as with pure analyses of Hegel's ideas (paragraph 2, sentence 4), both of which the author considers more useful. Thus, choice (A) is correct.

Choice (B) is incorrect: the author contrasts the biographies of statesmen and generals with those of philosophers but never offers an opinion on whether those biographies are more or less interesting. Choice (C) is wrong because philosopher biographies are only compared to Mill's autobiography, not philosopher autobiographies in general; also, the issue of satisfaction is, at best, a nebulous one. Choice (D) is too vague: philosopher biographies could be more informative or less informative than Mill's work. And since we don't know what informative means in this context, we have no grounds for making this inference. Choice (E) is incorrect because, at least from the evidence provided about Pinkard's Hegel biography (paragraph 3, sentence 2), philosopher biographies are books about the context in which philosophers wrote. So philosopher biographies cannot be compared, favorably or unfavorably, to themselves.

11. D

Choice (A) is incorrect because the author raises this issue but does not resolve it. We can eliminate choice (B) because the author never tries to convince the reader to read Hegel's writing. Choice (C) is a 180: the author criticizes, rather than defends, Pinkard's book. Finally, while the author touches on choice (E), it is buried in the details of the second paragraph and cannot be described as the passage's primary purpose. Choice (D) is exactly in line with the scope and purpose of the passage and is the credited answer.

12. E

In this paragraph, the author largely abandons the overall argument of the passage: it is devoted to details about Hegel that will inform and support the criticisms that follow. Choice (A) is incorrect because paragraph 2 focuses exclusively on Hegel. Choice (B) is incorrect because, while Hegel may be an exception, the author does not wish to avoid discussing him. Choice (C) is incorrect because the paragraph does not offer any defense of Hegel. Choice (D) is incorrect because its extreme language ("impossible") goes outside the scope of the passage; the author is concerned only with Pinkard's attempt to write about him. Choice (E), which matches our prediction, is the credited answer choice.

13. C

This part of the passage addresses what kinds of people make for good biography and what kinds of people do not. Quinton's remark illustrates Hegel's distance from figures who are more easily brought to life in print. Choice (C) is correct.

Choice (A) is incorrect because we know nothing about how Hegel or other philosophers were influenced by mentors. Choice (B) is incorrect because we learn nothing about Hegel's or others' social behavior. Choice (D) is incorrect because the passage does not focus on the process of researching a biography. Choice (E) is incorrect because it is far outside of the scope and does not seem at all to be an accurate rendering of "easily humanized."

CHAPTER TWELVE

Analytical Writing Assessment

The Analytical Writing Assessment (AWA) contains two essay assignments: *Present Your Perspective on an Issue* and *Analyze an Argument.* For the Issue essay (45 minutes), a sentence or paragraph that expresses an opinion on a topic of general interest will be presented. You'll be asked to respond to this opinion, communicating your own view of the issue presented. For the Argument essay (30 minutes), you will be presented with a paragraph that argues a certain point. Your essay should discuss how well reasoned you believe the argument is. For both essays, whether you agree or disagree with the claims presented is irrelevant; what matters is that you support your view with relevant examples and statements.

Each essay will be graded on a scale from 1–6. (A score of 0 means that your essay is off-topic.) This score is computed and reported separately from the multiple-choice section, and has no effect on your verbal, quantitative, or total score. The schools to which you are sending your GRE results may ask for a copy of your essay answers; however, your own copy of your score report will not include the completed text.

For the AWA, you will be evaluated on how well you:

- Organize, develop, and express your ideas about the argument presented
- Provide relevant supporting reasons and examples
- Control the elements of standard written English

Here are some proven strategies for scoring big on the AWA section of the GRE:

KAPLAN METHOD FOR ANALYTICAL WRITING

		Issue	Argument
Step 1:	Digest the issue/argument	2 minutes	2 minutes
Step 2:	Select the points you will make	5 minutes	7 minutes
Step 3:	Organize	1 minute	3 minutes
Step 4:	Write/type your essay	20 minutes	30 minutes
Step 5:	Proofread your work	2 minutes	3 minutes

KAPLAN'S 22 PRINCIPLES OF EFFECTIVE WRITING

1. Avoid wordiness
2. Don't be redundant
3. Avoid needless qualification
4. Do not write sentences just to fill up space
5. Avoid needless self-reference
6. Use the active voice
7. Avoid weak openings
8. Avoid needlessly vague language
9. Avoid clichés
10. Avoid jargon
11. Pay attention to subject-verb agreement
12. Pay attention to modification
13. Use pronouns carefully
14. Use parallelism carefully
15. Do not shift narrative voice
16. Avoid slang and colloquialisms
17. Watch out for sentence fragments and run-on sentences
18. Use commas correctly
19. Use semicolons correctly
20. Use colons correctly
21. Use hyphens and dashes correctly
22. Use the apostrophe correctly

SIX TIPS FOR WRITING A "6" ESSAY

Remember: your essay is not expected to be perfect. You can still get a 6 and have a few minor errors.

1. Keep sight of your goal: to demonstrate that you can think logically and communicate clearly.

2. Use language effectively; watch for words that add nothing to the sentence.

3. Keep your word choice, sentence structure, and argument simple (but not simplistic).

4. Resist the temptation to use inflated language in your essays; big words that don't fit the tone or context of your essays won't impress anyone.

5. Be strong and convincing in your choice of arguments, words, and sentence style.

6. Don't worry too much about making minor mistakes.

Be sure to check out www.gre.org/stuwrit.html for sample essay prompts.

The remainder of this chapter includes two sample prompts and essays for both the Issue and Argument writing assignments.

You will notice the use of strong transitions, logical organization, and effective word choice in the sample essays. All of these factors contribute to their receipt of a top score.

PRESENT YOUR PERSPECTIVE ON AN ISSUE

(45 Minutes)

Present your perspective on the issue below, using relevant reasons and/or examples to support your views.

> "Ailing patients should have easy access to their doctor's history with similarly afflicted patients, so that the ailing patients may better determine whether the doctor is competent to treat their medical condition."

_____

_____

_____

_____

_____

_____

_____

_____

_____

_____

_____

_____

ANALYSIS OF AN ARGUMENT

(30 Minutes)

Discuss how well reasoned you find this argument.

The following appeared in a memorandum written by the president of Tempo Media, a small literary agency:

"Good customer service equals good business. All employees should respond to our clients' needs as quickly as possible, placing this aspect of your jobs above all else. If a customer or client contacts you with a question, drop everything and get back to them as soon as possible. This level of responsiveness will increase sales because satisfied clients will increase our profile in the literary marketplace, bringing in more clients, and satisfied customers will create a word-of-mouth buzz about our books, leading to more sales."

_____

_____

_____

_____

_____

_____

_____

_____

_____

_____

_____

SAMPLE ISSUE ESSAY (SCORE 6)

Present your perspective on the issue below, using relevant reasons and/or examples to support your views.

> "Ailing patients should have easy access to their doctor's history with similarly afflicted patients, so that the ailing patients may better determine whether the doctor is competent to treat their medical condition."

On the surface, the idea that ill patients should have access to their doctors' histories of treating people with similar ailments seems to be an appealing idea. Free access to information is one of the cornerstones of our society, and when it comes to deciding where to buy a used car or to take your dry cleaning, you want to have as much information about the providers of these services as possible. But shopping for a health-care provider is very different. Whether or not someone is a good doctor cannot be adequately represented by facts and figures about their patients. Although having access to a doctor's history would not be detrimental, careful consideration of the subtleties surrounding medical treatment reveals that selecting a doctor solely based on their records on paper would not be a wise course of action.

If you were preparing to buy a used car, you would research the reputations of local car dealers and whether the type of car you were interested in was reliable and a good value. It would seem that you could ask the same types of questions about doctors and their treatment methods in order to make a more informed decision about who to choose as your physician. But medical treatment is a different kind of service than used car dealing. For one thing, illness can manifest itself very differently in different patients. Just because an illness is called by the same name (colon cancer, for example), does not mean that every patient's colon cancer will progress in exactly the same way as another's. Medicines and treatment plans that work for one patient's illness may not be effective for another patient with a similar affliction. Just because Patient A with colon cancer survived doesn't mean that Patient B would too.

And what if Patient A did die from her disease? That fact alone is not enough information to disqualify her doctor from treating other cancer patients. Doctors lose patients; it's inevitable. More relevant factors to consider would be whether or not the deceased patient suffered, if she lived longer than expected, and if the doctor was attentive to her needs. But it would be very difficult for an average prospective patient to find out any of this information from available patient data.

Most prospective patients are not medical experts, and access to a doctor's history would probably not mean much to them. It would be more useful for a prospective patient to interview people a doctor treated previously, or to read their personal accounts of their relationship with their doctor to find out what type of caregiver a doctor is. But most people do not volunteer their stories in this way, and this is not the kind of data one finds in a medical history. Patients also have rights to privacy that would prevent many personal details from being revealed in a history available to the general public, making it even more difficult for an outsider to judge a doctor's efficacy based on this type of source. Medical review boards exist to regulate the ethical practice of medicine, and if a doctor has done something truly incompetent which endangered a patient's life, that doctor would be barred from practicing medicine. Those kinds of judgments are best left to medical experts.

While having a doctor's history available would not be a bad thing, neither should it be considered the best way to choose a doctor. It makes more sense to base the choice of a doctor on referrals from other physicians, recommendations from friends, and the formation of an opinion about the doctor through personal interactions. When choosing a physician, the comfort level and trust between individual patients and doctors should be paramount.

SAMPLE ARGUMENT ESSAY (SCORE 6)

Discuss how well reasoned you find this argument.

The following appeared in a memorandum written by the president of Tempo Media, a small literary agency:

"Good customer service equals good business. All employees should respond to our clients' needs as quickly as possible, placing this aspect of your jobs above all else. If a customer or client contacts you with a question, drop everything and get back to them as soon as possible. This level of responsiveness will increase sales because satisfied clients will increase our profile in the literary marketplace, bringing in more clients, and satisfied customers will create a word-of-mouth buzz about our books, leading to more sales."

The president of Tempo Media is making a big leap in her opening sentence. Although good customer service is an important component of good business practice, customer service alone is not enough to guarantee success. Therefore, the president had based her entire argument on faulty logic. In addition, poor reasoning, a lack of substantiating evidence, and a reliance on obscure terminology weaken the message of the memo.

A small literary agency such as Tempo Media will have to do a number of things in order increase sales, which is the stated goal of the company's president. Responsive customer service is one of them, but the staff must also be concerned with representing excellent products, effective marketing, and maintaining their workplace efficiency. If all the employees of the company "drop everything" to attend to customer service, as the president suggests, other aspects of the employees' responsibilities will surely suffer. Therefore, even in a small company it makes sense to designate a few people to deal with customer relations issues so that everyone else can concentrate on his or her area of expertise without the distraction of constant interruptions. The scenario the president outlines encourages disorganization, a lack of focus and may even contribute to a decline in the quality of the employees' work.

The president's assumption that "satisfied clients will increase our profile in the literary marketplace, bringing in more clients, and satisfied customers will create a word-of-mouth buzz about our books, leading to more sales" is also problematic. The president does not offer any evidence that, in fact, satisfying clients and customers will lead directly to increased sales. Although it cannot be a bad thing for a company to establish a reputation for good customer service, that alone may not be enough to increase the company's sales. If the president referred to studies showing a correlation between having a high profile in the marketplace and attracting more clients, her argument would be greatly improved. Likewise, any proof that word-of-mouth buzz generates more sales would also go a long way towards substantiating the president's claims.

Another problem with the president's argument is her tendency to use certain terms without making their meanings clear. It would strengthen the president's position if she defined exactly who the clients and customers of the literary agency are, what she means by "the literary marketplace," and "word-of-mouth buzz." Her reliance on these vague phrases to support her position only serves to create the impression that her argument does not make a lot of sense.

Although the president of Tempo Media undoubtedly has her company's best interest in mind, the memo presented here does not offer an adequately supported line of reasoning for the recommended course of action. A close examination reveals significant lapses in the logic of the president's position, undermining her argument that customer service should be the primary focus of each of her employees.

PRESENT YOUR PERSPECTIVE ON AN ISSUE

(45 Minutes)

Present your perspective on the issue below, using relevant reasons and/or examples to support your views.

"People that have never created a work of art are unqualified to criticize a work of art."

_____

_____

_____

_____

_____

_____

_____

_____

_____

_____

_____

_____

_____

ANALYSIS OF AN ARGUMENT

(30 Minutes)

Discuss how well reasoned you find this argument.

The following appeared in a report submitted for discussion at the board meeting of the Williamstown Icecats, a minor league hockey team:

"Our attendance levels have been falling to the point where we have 5,000 fewer fans per game than we did last season. As everyone here knows, last year the owner of the Polar Bears moved his hockey team to Williamstown and began charging less than we charge for tickets, clearly the cause of our low attendance. Our only hope of raising attendance is to lower our prices so our tickets are cheaper than Polar Bears tickets."

_____

_____

_____

_____

_____

_____

_____

_____

_____

_____

_____

_____

SAMPLE ISSUE ESSAY (SCORE 6)

Present your perspective on the issue below, using relevant reasons and/or examples to support your views.

> "People that have never created a work of art are unqualified to criticize a work of art."

The assumption that people who are not themselves artists are unqualified to criticize art is entirely untrue. One of the basic functions of art in our society is to elicit reactions from the public. Art is created for public consumption and will inevitably be criticized by anyone, artists and laypersons alike, who experience it.

Critics, often, are not unfamiliar with the artistic genre they cover. Conversely, they are usually trained in their fields, often studying and surrounding themselves with the very art form they criticize. Learning to appreciate an art form and to recognize its function in the field (as well as in the world at large), is a legitimate course of study and career choice. In fact, many universities offer critical theory degree programs and courses in art appreciation covering everything from film studies to music appreciation to art history. Essentially, most graduate programs in the arts and humanities prepare students to become art critics.

Of course, it does make for a more relevant and insightful review of the critic has some formal training (or at least some exposure to what formal training entails). Well-trained critics acquire a breadth and depth of knowledge of not only the field and art form, but of relevant artists and significant movements or periods in the field.

If people that experience and study art are not "qualified" to react to, process, and articulate their opinions about art, then who is? If only painters could react to fellow painters' works, the art world would become insular and inaccessible, which could lead to the demise of public interest and funding. In fact, none of our most famous film critics has ever made a film: not Janet Maslin (<u>the New York Times</u>), not Roger Ebert (<u>Chicago Sun-Times</u>), not David Denby of <u>the New Yorker</u>.

Part of the power and relevance of art is to involve interested parties in the art world. Those who support art contribute greatly to make the art world possible and sustainable, through financial contributions and the establishment of artistic foundations and academic art programs. These people, arguably as much as artists themselves, help bolster a popular interest in the arts. Because of this, they have a right to interpret whatever art they observe.

Furthermore, in this society, we hold fast to our constitutional freedom of speech. If we restrict who is "allowed" to criticize art (or anything else, for that matter), we will restrict the very fabric of our society. What's next — the banning of Oprah's book club and neighborhood book groups informally critiquing Jane Austen? Artists and their critics have a long-standing relationship fraught with tension, which in and of itself contributes to the vitality and relevance of art. Like it or not, art will always be critiqued by trained critics and the general public alike.

SAMPLE ARGUMENT ESSAY (SCORE 6)

Discuss how well reasoned you find this argument.

The following appeared in a report submitted for discussion at the board meeting of the Williamstown Icecats, a minor league hockey team:

"Our attendance levels have been falling to the point where we have 5,000 fewer fans per game than we did last season. As everyone here knows, last year the owner of the Polar Bears moved his hockey team to Williamstown and began charging less than we charge for tickets, clearly the cause of our low attendance. Our only hope of raising attendance is to lower our prices so our tickets are cheaper than Polar Bears tickets."

This report submitted at the Williamstown Icecats board meeting blames the recent drop in attendance at Icecats games on the arrival of a new hockey team in town which charges less for tickets to its games. Although the cheaper price of the Polar Bears' tickets may be a factor in the attendance decline at Icecats games, the members of the board would be unwise to assume the issue can be easily resolved by lowering their own ticket prices, since the report fails to examine other issues that may be affecting the turnout at Icecats' games. Furthermore, the report suffers from reliance on poorly defined terms and logical leaps of faith without adequate supporting information.

The report blames the Icecats' failure to attract as large an audience as last season on the fact that the Polar Bears are charging less for their tickets than the Icecats. However, other factors may be contributing to the Icecats' diminishing fan base. The Icecats might be having terrible season, while the Polar Bears could be winning. Perhaps the Icecats have lost their star players to the Polar Bears team. The report also does not mention if the Polar Bears are in the same hockey league as the Icecats. If the Polar Bears are a major league team, that could also contribute to their popularity. In addition, the report does not consider factors outside of hockey that could be affecting attendance. Maybe Williamstown is having a particularly severe winter, causing people to go out less. Or perhaps the town is suffering from an economic slump or a general decline in population.

The report also suffers from a failure to adequately detail its supporting arguments. It states that the Polar Bears' owner charges "less" for his tickets, but it does not say how much less. If the price difference is negligible, the Icecats should look elsewhere for an explanation for their falling attendance. The report would also do well to mention the total number of tickets it is selling per game instead of just that there are "5,000 fewer fans per game." Without an idea of the total ticket sales, it is difficult to assess the net loss the team is suffering. It could also be that last year's large crowds were an anomaly, since no long-term attendance statistics are provided in the report.

In order to bolster the claim that the Icecats loss of 5,000 fans per game can be entirely fixed on the Polar Bears' cheaper tickets, the report should offer some evidence that shows a direct link, such as a study showing that people think the Icecats' tickets are too expensive, or a poll of attendees of Polar Bears' games that establishes that they once went to the Icecats' games but changed their loyalties based entirely on the relative cost of the tickets. The report as it stands now has too many assumptions and logical fallacies to be taken seriously by the board. If they were to act on the advice of the report and lower ticket prices, they might well find they have not addressed the real cause of the problem and, in turn, exacerbate the organization's financial woes.